ETHEREAL SHADOWS

Communication and Power in Contemporary Italy

———————— • ————————

Franco "Bifo" Berardi Marco Jacquemet Gianfranco Vitali

translated by Jessica Otey

AUTONOMEDIA

NEW YORK

Ethereal Shadows

Cover and Book Design by R&S Media

Autonomedia
PO Box 568 Williamsburgh Station
Brooklyn, NY 11211-0568 USA

www.autonomedia.org
info@autonomedia.org

This publication is made possible in part with public funds
from the New York State Council on the Arts, a state agency.

NYSCA
New York State Council on the Arts

Contents

Preface

This project has a long history. We started thinking about it in late spring 1994 when we witnessed the takeover of Italian politics by a motley crew of racists, former fascists and Mafia-like businessmen, led by Silvio Berlusconi, a media mogul with a funny look and a murky past. This motley crew had just won the national elections on March 27, due in part to a savvy use of the media and in part to the demise of the leftist social movements that had shaped Italy since the late 1960s. This marked the first time that media and political power had come together in such a shameless and powerful combination. We deemed it necessary to investigate this phenomenon in depth. The relationship between media, politics and society had always been at the center of our concerns as citizens, activists and researchers. The political events in 1994 provided us with concrete evidence for some of our theoretical hypotheses and literary dystopias on the devolution of Italian politics and society. In the summer and fall of that year we worked on a first draft of this book, which we called "Cyberfascism and Italian Karaoke."

The prefix "cyber" had become in those years a buzzword in media and cultural studies. It referred to new media technologies, a radicalized social imaginary and transformed class relations—in other words, all the marvels of the cyberpunk world imagined by William Gibson in *Neuromancer*. By hyphenating it with "fascism" we wanted to evoke not-so-distant Italian memories, which pointed to the violent and intolerant tendencies of an all-controlling Big Brother, able this time to use his telematic power to discipline and rule. But what about "Italian karaoke"? During one of his periodic visits prior to the 1994 elections, Marco, who had left Italy many years before, had been struck by the fact that the Italian piazzas were no longer filled by crowds voicing their political conviction and rebellion, but by thousands of people watching the performance on a big stage of a dozen amateur actors who lip-synched and moved to the tunes of 1970s songs. Karaoke had landed in Italy with a twist: a spectacular, popular dimension promoted by Berlusconi's networks, which broadcasted in prime time this spectacle of conformity and media protagonism. This version of karaoke seemed an apt metaphor for Berlusconi's first government, which seemed to us shaped by a similar mixture of mimicry and tele-transmission, conformism and lack of social and political responsibility.

Soon after, we realized that the emerging regime could not match the authoritarian hold of historical fascism. Its ideological roots were too shallow and it was unable to transform its media power into a political machine. In fact, after just nine months in power, Berlusconi's government collapsed. We welcomed the turn of events and set our book project aside.

However, we maintained our concern about the state of Italian democracy. The level of political engagement that had characterized Italy in the late 1960s and 1970s had come to an end, leaving in its wake a center-left coalition unable to change the social and cultural conditions engineered by twenty years of neoliberal policies and a growing media monopoly. In the new millennium, Berlusconi's media and political machine resurfaced with a vengeance, this time with deeper roots and stronger structures. On May 13, 2001, Berlusconi won the national elections again. This time he not only went the distance, but he almost managed to repeat the feat in 2006, despite his abysmal record in government.

Meanwhile, new oppositional social actors had emerged on the political scene on November 30, 1999, during anti-globalization riots against the World Trade Organization's meeting in Seattle. After Berlusconi was elected, his mediacentric political regime found itself contending with the Italian offshoot of this new force: political, cultural and media networks able to counter the monopolistic media agenda and neoliberal project promoted by the government. These networks, whose media practices came to be known in Italy and abroad as "media activism," were at the same time both local and global: they inspired people to meet and fill the streets in mass demonstrations by organizing through the means of global communication, including computer networks, airwaves and satellite transmissions.

At that point, we reopened the drawer and reread our old materials, finding them at times naïve but prophetic. With the help of our translator, Jessica Otey, we cut out some of the naïveties, edited with the English-speaking world in mind, and added new sections documenting not only the increasingly explicit development of the mediacentric regime, but also the emergence of the contrasting voice of Italian media activism. Our main objective in this rewrite was to balance our critique of Berlusconi's mediated regime with an analysis of the alternatives.

This book now has two parts. In the first half, we focus on the current Italian "videocracy," documenting the emergence of the first Italian media mogul, Silvio Berlusconi, and his rise to political power. In the second half, we explore Italian "media activism" through three case studies: a discussion of the first autonomous free radio station, Radio Alice (which broadcasted in Bologna between 1977 and 1979); a review of Italian Internet activism, focusing on the site rekombinant.org (created in 2000); and finally a chronicle of the emergence of OrfeoTV in 2002, the first Italian example of an illegal micro-TV station. The latter case provided the inspiration for the title.

Micro-TV stations like OrfeoTV operate in small areas, technically called "shadow zones," where the frequency of a national broadcast cannot be picked up because of natural or human-made obstacles. In these shadows, small activist outfits can superimpose their signal over the broadcasts of a national network (for example, OrfeoTV uses a shadow zone on the frequency assigned to MTV Italy). OrfeoTV served as inspiration for the creation of more than a hundred micro-TV stations throughout Italy that later went on to form Telestreet, a national network of micro-broadcasters sharing equipment and skills and providing each other with technical and political support.

Italy has become a political laboratory for worrisome but intriguing trends in society and media politics—trends that have been seen in incipient form in many other parts of the world. What is happening in Italy is relevant for the future of democracy all over the world. In this book we engage with key questions relating to media politics: Are media outlets destined to become huge conglomerates and monopolies in the hands of people eager to enter the political arena for personal advantage? What are the social and political consequences of this marriage of media and politics? How can concerned citizens resist these media and political monopolies? How is the public space of communication going to be used in the future?

The struggle in Italy between teledictatorship and media activism is in full swing. We call this analysis of media struggle *Ethereal Shadows*, to depict a mediascape where we sense both the ghost of a mediacentric political regime and the bodies of a gathering multitude, the totalitarian media oppression but also the communicative practices of a social body trying to aggregate itself through the emission of ethereal signs.

—*Sant'Angelo d'Ischia, July 10, 2006*

INTRODUCTION

The year 2002 was a palindrome of ill times—and a typical example of what it meant to live under Berlusconi's regime: the year started badly and ended badly. It started with the world waiting for imminent economic and military catastrophe. For the last two years, Italy had been enthralled by the spectacle of the political and economic success and unbounded optimism of its prime minister, media mogul Silvio Berlusconi. Yet Censis, an institute for the study of social trends, found Italians to be listless, afraid, distrustful of the future, uncertain of their chances and cynical. Italy was a country running on empty. Its most important industrial company, Fiat, was on the brink of collapse. The automobile conglomerate, which for the last century has clogged every single street and square of the medieval and Renaissance towns of *il Bel Paese* [the beautiful country] with its cars, announced thousands of layoffs in all its plants, from Turin to Sicily. The Berlusconi government's budget for 2003 called for severe cuts in public education and healthcare in order to push forward with its privatization plans and tax cuts. Inflation, due in part to the conversion to the Euro, was on the rise. Salaries were frozen and purchasing power decreased every month. Thanks to a recent law on immigration, it became possible to arrest people without work visas. Off the shores of the beautiful beaches of Southern Italy, many young Africans, Kurds and Pakistanis drowned trying to ford the moat surrounding Fortress Europe. Outside of Italy, while the recession was hitting all Western economies hard, the President of the United States threatened war and massacre. In Chechnya, Palestine, Indonesia, the Philippines, Venezuela, Colombia and other hot spots, there was an epidemic of suicide bombings, car bombs and deadly reprisals.

Just before Christmas, the Pope, tired and sickly, announced with slurred words that God had withdrawn from the world, choosing to remain silent, estranged from the destiny of humankind: the divinity was disgusted by human deeds.

Only a sanitized version of these events reached Italian TV screens. This news was filtered through national media outlets, almost all of which were owned or controlled by Berlusconi, who was aptly nicknamed *Sua Emittenza* (a play on the honorific *Sua Eminenza* [His Eminence] and *emittenza* [broadcasting]). The Eminence of Broadcasting would not allow any harsh realities to impinge upon his world. Political talking heads were carefully selected, and those who might express dangerous opinions were purged.

Since the elections in 2001, the main feature of Berlusconi's regime had become its ability to produce simulated reality, to present on TV a world existing only in the dreams of the prime minister. Meanwhile, Italy has come to represent the clearest example to date of the society of the hyperspectacle, in which television is the most consumed cultural product and the imaginary energies of the viewers are channeled away from real life to fill the dreamlike world of spectacle. The overwhelming majority of Italians get their news solely from the TV screen. After more than twenty years of an unremitting barrage of television, Italian consumption of print media has dropped to the lowest level in Europe: in 2002, only one Italian out of five visited a bookstore, and only one out of ten bought a newspaper regularly (Censis 2002).

Berlusconi came to politics late in life. He acquired his wealth as a media executive, rising through the ranks of marketing and sales departments. He learned to project a persona of sugary sentiment and feel-good attitudes. His political style consisted of smiling a lot, telling jokes, making astonishing promises and blaming somebody else, anybody, when things went wrong. His media outlets portrayed him as a man whose good plans were held back by evil communists, whom he saw hidden everywhere, busily scheming to sabotage his paradise. As a result, while the Italian economy headed for disaster, Berlusconi never stopped flashing his dazzling smile, soothing his subjects with encouraging and benevolent words. Yet the cost of living increased considerably under his watch, and this fact cannot be hidden behind media simulations or communist conspiracies. Italian consumers had become nervous and reluctant to buy, even though the television networks (all owned or controlled by Berlusconi) every day exhorted them to spend and consume. Regardless of the vigilant efforts of media professionals to dull the harsh facts, the state of the world has infiltrated Italians' social imagination, coloring it in depressing hues.

Under Berlusconi, Italy has experienced the ultimate offensive of the aggressive, neoliberal society of the hyperspectacle against human life and the general intellect; a great leap forward in the colonization of the social mind. The Italian situation has to be understood as the end result of twenty-five years of neoliberal ideology and practice, as a by-product of the processes of centralization and monopolization of the mediascape, and, finally, as a macroscopic sign of the formation of a global neo-Mafia, whose social contours have little to do with the old-fashioned, Sicilian-based Mafia.

Neoliberal policy burst onto the Italian scene in the 1970s under the banner of "deregulation." This was not bad in itself. When the controls imposed on markets are inadequate to the needs of society, deregulation is sometimes good. But neoliberal deregulation meant to destroy any social control of the economy in order to impose the limitless law of profit. This has favored a small and aggressive minority of deregulating capitalists, who have seized control of the means of producing semiocapital. This aggressive minority has imposed its will on the world, without regard for the consequences.

In our view, this evolution helps explain what has happened in Italy since the late 1970s. In this country, an aggressive, neoliberal bourgeoisie has taken advantage of a long tradition of the ruling class's mastery of political expediency to produce a simulacrum of authority, democracy and wealth.

At times, Italy has been considered a 'culturally backward' society. Its modernization has long appeared incomplete. The Protestant Reformation that shaped the spirit of modern capitalism in Northern Europe never reached Italy. On the other hand, the legacy of the Counter-Reformation turned Italy into a country where illegalities flourish, corruption runs rampant and lies and flattery are expected behavior—these are the virtues of late-modern capitalism.

A few Italian businessmen have become wealthy by manipulating and controlling access to communication—the dominant tool of production in a postindustrial economy. Berlusconi is one of these men—actually the richest of all them—and decided to use his wealth to run for political office. Due in part to the incredible power accumulated by Berlusconi's financial and media conglomerate, Fininvest, on May 13, 2001, he seized political power with the help of his allies: the former fascist party (now renamed *Alleanza Nazionale* [AN, National Alliance]); the racist party from Northern Italy, *Lega Nord* [LN, Northern League]; and the *Centro Cristiano Democratico* [CCD, Christian Democratic Center], the right-wing offshoot of the disgraced *Democrazia Cristiana* [DC, Christian Democracy], the party that ruled Italy from 1945 to 1994 until it collapsed under the weight of the corruption scandal knows as *Tangentopoli* [Kickback City].

This was the second time in a decade that the right-wing parties won big. The first time, in 1994, the right-wing coalition had not managed to hold on to power very long: after nine months of internecine struggles, Berlusconi's government imploded. In special national elections in 1996, the Right was defeated by a center-left coalition led by Romano Prodi, a reformed Christian Democrat who would later become the President of the European Union. During the five years of its mandate, the center-left government showed a disarming lack of vision and cultural subalternity to the politics of neoliberalism. As a result, by the time of the 2001 national elections, a disillusioned and dispirited electorate was ready to not renew its mandate.

In addition, in 2001, the lackluster Prodi administration had to contend with a more focused, better groomed, and highly motivated Berlusconi. Despite the fact that his personal and business affairs were increasingly under the scrutiny of various judges in different Italian courtrooms, Berlusconi invested a huge amount of money in an effective campaign of political advertising, and obtained a narrow victory over the center-left. Due to a revamped electoral system, this narrow victory translated into a strong majority in Parliament. Berlusconi quickly went to work settling old scores, and placing his people in all the available public offices.

Once Berlusconi, owner of three TV networks, stepped into power, the public television network (RAI-TV) was taken over by his cohort of yes-men. Until that point, RAI had competed against his Mediaset network, thus making it within Berlusconi's own cultural and economic interests to destroy it. In the spring of 2002, the attack on RAI reached its peak when Berlusconi (in a speech made during a trip to Bulgaria) announced that RAI had to rid itself of Michele Santoro and Enzo Biagi, two very popular television personalities who had assumed dissident stances towards Berlusconi's regime. Despite protests from the Italian intelligentsia, the executives of the Administrative Council of RAI, loyal to Berlusconi, erased the two dissidents from the programming schedule. There were two consequences: the first was the silencing of two very different critical voices (the populist and activist voice of Santoro, and the moderate and self-righteous one of Biagi). The second (and more important) consequence was that two programs with huge audiences—that is, programs that were taking potential advertising revenues from Berlusconi's Mediaset— were eliminated. There were many more cases of Berlusconi's appalling fiat, and by the end of 2002 the whole range of the Italian infosphere (six national TV networks, and the majority of print media) had been taken over by Berlusconi and his crew. For the first time in the history of Italian television, one of Mediaset's channels, Canale 5, became the most watched in Italy, leaving behind the flagship channel of state television, RAI Uno.

None of this happened without fierce opposition from a growing sector of public opinion. Parliamentary opposition to the many legislative proposals designed to serve Berlusconi's self-interest was extremely strong. Center-left parliamentarians denounced the subordination of the state to the interests of an individual and a small coterie of businessmen in all possible ways. A broad movement developed in Milan, Rome and Florence against the illegality driving the government's actions, such as the arrogant subjection of RAI. One portion of this movement was led by director Nanni Moretti, a figure of great prestige in Italian cinema who had already denounced the corruption of the governments of Tangentopoli with the film *Portaborse*. Nearly a million people were brought onto the streets of Rome and occupied the central squares of numerous cities with peaceful and choreographic human chains. They represented the more moderate element of the movement that opposed the center-right government: concerned citizens, still linked to the center-left coalition, who regarded the center-right government as an abnormal phenomenon linked to the Mafia-like particularity of the Italian situation, and hoped for a return to democratic rule without substantial changes to the economic and social system.

In Italy, as in many other countries in the world, a broader and more variegated movement has developed that identifies with a social criticism of capitalist globalization and the platform of the Social Forums. This movement has brought hundreds of thousands of young people into the streets to protest against the racism of the migration laws, as well as against terrorism and war. The first test of the resistance against the Berlusconi government came in July 2001, with the mobilization in

Genoa against the G8 summit. On three consecutive days, hundreds of thousands of people—not only the young—occupied the streets of the city, shouting their opposition to neoliberal policies around the world and in Italy. The Italian police decided to use force to contain these marches and unrelentingly charged the demonstrators. During the second day of protests, a young man by the name of Carlo Giuliani was killed by a young military policeman who was allegedly panicking about his own safety. In subsequent sweeps, scores of people, including numerous media activists, were tortured, mistreated, injured and humiliated. In the days following the police violence in Genoa, a movement of hundreds of thousands of people again took to the streets in many Italian cities to protest.

This movement continued to expand in subsequent months, despite the catastrophic twist that 9/11 stamped on world politics. In Rome, on November 10, 2001, a hundred thousand people demonstrated against the American war in Afghanistan and against the warmongering fanaticism of the Berlusconi government. On January 15, 2002, a hundred and fifty thousand people demonstrated against a new anti-immigration law in Rome, calling for the right of free circulation for all migrants. Then, on March 23, once again in Rome, the Confederazione Generale Italiana del Lavoro, the biggest trade union in the country, called on workers to demonstrate against the government's attack on their rights at work. Three million people answered the call, and Rome witnessed its biggest demonstration since 1945. Once again, the opposition movement set a date in Florence for three days of discussion about a social Europe, and called a demonstration for November 9, 2002 against permanent war and neoliberal policies. A million people answered this call, and a huge crowd screaming slogans of peace occupied the city for the whole day. Lastly, on February 15, 2003, a million people filled the streets of Rome in a powerful demonstration against the war in Iraq.

But this enormous and protracted political uprising, accompanied by strikes, demonstrations and protests in every city of Italy, did not succeed in bending the will of the media dictator and his political cohorts. The demonstrations of November 10, 2001 and February 15, 2003 did not force even a pause in the belligerent war machine of the Italian government. Nor did January 15 induce any modification in the anti-immigration law. The three million people who demonstrated with the trade union did not manage to convince the government to modify any aspect of its legislative agenda against workers' rights. The opposition to Berlusconi—and more broadly, to neoliberal and aggressive policies—simply exhausted itself, dissipating in rivulets of discontent, frustration and impotence.

We believe this movement needs new social practices in order to overthrow a despotic regime that combines hard methods of control with softer means of manufactured consent. We are convinced that future mobilizations need to be principally media-centered.

In Italy, television is one of the main sources of the regime's power. As Italy's clownish dictator has seized control of the whole of the mediascape, many think that his power is going to be indestructible, but this may not be the case. While communication has shaped and is still shaping the regime, it has also been the place where a fierce battle has been fought since the 1970s between ruling classes and social movements. Italy has a strong tradition of resistance to authoritarian forms of communication. Media activism has taken many forms, actions and practices. It has spread from radio to television and the Internet. Since the Seattle riots against the World Trade Organization summit in November 1999, a new global movement has emerged that practices the spread of independent media and the convergence from below of videostreaming, digital networks and alternative virtual communities. Antagonistic net culture and media activism have started a process that may eventually destroy the overwhelming power of the television and its masters.

This movement, whose culture and perspectives we will discuss in the second half of this book, needs to become the central component of the opposition to Berlusconi's regime. As we will argue in the following pages, this movement marks the beginning of a new consciousness: the social forces of science, technology and communication have begun to claim independence from the rule of profit. In Italy, an increasing number of people working in media production are trying to organize themselves independently from the media conglomerates.

Media politics will be the field where the battle for freedom and democracy will be fought. This will be a battle of the media activists against the hold of a few corporations on the shaping of the social imagination, and for the creation of an autonomous social space for the self-organization of intellectual energies.

Media activism—the independent organization of means of communication—has been increasing in recent years, with the diffusion of the Internet and the creation of small outfits using every means of communication technology, from the printed word to video, radio and the Web. Media activism seeks to contest domination of the social mind, to broaden spaces of cultural self-organization and to give life to social networks for the sharing of skills and knowledge. It aims to redirect mental time, energy and intellectual resources away from televisual consumption and assign it to discursive, imaginary, ideological and desiring autonomous media production.

Media activism has spread widely, mobilizing within cultural environments that have formed all over the planet against the devastation wreaked by global corporations and the hypercapitalist policies pursued by international organizations of global government (such as the WTO, the IMF, the World Bank and so on). Since the Seattle uprising, media activists have had a central role in the organization of the protest movement. They have astutely used global data transmission networks to create autonomous spaces for discussion and proposals—a kind of permanent planetary media assemblage. They have created environments like Indymedia to function as instruments of capillary information and global coordination. But media activists have not limited themselves only to making the circulation of information possible, they have also experimented with a principle of sharing resources that prefigures the possibility of a society liberated from the economic obsession with profit and privatization; thereby affirming the principles of open source content, file sharing and media cooperation as a new paradigm for the production of the social imagination.

This movement is founded on the mass diffusion of cognitive, technological, scientific and creative competencies. During the past few decades, we have witnessed the emergence of a new social class on a planetary scale. We would like to call this class the *cognitariat*, because it possesses an extremely high capacity for cognitive production but has marginal economic and political power. Like the proletariat of the industrial era, it is constrained to sell its capacities to those who hold capital. This social class was created through mass education, student movements, the computer revolution and the proliferation of the Internet. It possesses the necessary competencies to make the social factory function, to make progress on the technical level and to provide for the material and spiritual needs of humanity, but finds itself at work within the social conditions determined by the private appropriation of the products of intellectual labor. Media activism questions the principle of privatization of the products of intellectual labor on the specific terrain of communication, replacing it with the principles of unrestrained proliferation, free access and sharing.

During the 1980s, a variety of new conditions for the production and transmission of information were set in motion, such as: the widespread dissemination of information through every possible communicative channel; the virtualization of printing techniques; the proliferation of electronically produced images; and the globalization of news services. Because of this overload of images, information and simulation, opinion-making—meant as *doxa*—lost an identifiable core and talking heads became redundant; decision-making mechanisms were no longer determined by a single hegemonic force and tended to shatter into many "special interests."

During this period, television was the medium for the reception of events separated from the viewer. Now we are faced with the evolution of the television medium into two possible scenarios: neo-TV and post-TV. Neo-TV is the medium for the production/authentification of events through the mediatization (that is, the passive mobilization) of the viewer. Post-TV is the reticular structure for the construction and multiplication of simulated realities by digitalized entities belonging to virtual communities. Television brought the world into the experiential domain of the viewer. Neo-TV brings the viewer into a simulated, mesmerizing and totalitarian world. Post-TV could potentially lead out of this totalitarian world through the formation of libertarian, voluntary and temporary communities.

The entire world is witnessing the clash between the hyperspectacular and simulated machine of neo-TV networks and the digital archipelago of post-TV independent outfits. The outcome of this struggle is uncertain, depending as it does on the political conditions of technological developments and the political decisions regarding the production, management and use of electronic interfaces.

Italian media activism, and in particular the experience of Telestreet (the network of local micro-television stations broadcasting without license over a very limited area; see chapter 5), is simultaneously engaged in a political and cultural struggle. It needs to make a political statement against Berlusconi's media regime, but it is also trying to build new communicative tools able to link media production with the everyday, concrete and local practices of both media producers and consumers. In other words, it is *doing* politics through media production.

The conditions of Italian media democracy worry many European countries. The international press, the French and German in particular, does not hide its perplexity—and in some cases open hostility—toward a government led by a media magnate in collaboration with reactionary and revanchist forces. Their concerns are largely justified, even if such reactions risk interpreting the Italian situation in obsolete terms, according to the formulae and stereotypes of the early twentieth century.

In reality, the Berlusconi regime was formed with an original mix of cultural elements of a libertarian derivation, a repackaging of the classic clientele or Mafia model, and a postmodern form of manufacturing consent. The Italian Right in those years knew how to translate the desire for social innovation, transformation and liberation of production into political capital—a move the Left was not able to replicate. The innovation of the center-right regime lay essentially in a simultaneously arrogant and ingenious form of videocracy, in the experimentation with a model founded on the domination of the media landscape, on the monopoly of television, advertising and the entire information system. Given its history and theatrical inclination, Italy seemed predisposed to be the first site of a regime founded on the domination of the media landscape—that is, one based on the domination of the social imagination. Italian society as a whole had undergone an anthropological and cognitive change in the course of two decades of Fininvest's media domination. This mutation produced a structural change in the infosphere and in the strategies of social communication.

Italy made its transition into the postindustrial era in the last few decades, entering the integrated planetary cyberspace. But this transition took place under the sign of conformist homogenization of television, and not under the sign of the Internet, which in Italy initially produced relatively few changes on the cultural and imaginary levels. By cyberspace we mean the collective field of information and thought exchanged between all sentient beings interacting by electronic means. This is a domain in which the truth of experience no longer coincides with the place in which it takes place. The diffusion of video technologies, the digitalization of social representation and language, and the correlated transformation of productive processes and social interactions are the basic practices of this changing world.

In the last few decades, digital technology has contributed to a profound mutation in the communicative and sociocultural environment. The human organism has been catapulted into a new phenomenological domain. It is our claim that the postmodern political landscape arises from this cognitive, psychic and anthropological change that humanity appears to be undergoing. This change impacts the most elementary forms of human activity: perception, language, learning, memory and cognitive representation. As a result of this mutation, the analytic categories based on perceptive and interpretative models proper to modernity, and thus also its forms of political action, have little chance of surviving. The categories used by modern political thought to develop the concept of democracy are no longer valid. Traditional political power (that is, representative democracy) is increasingly unable to face this mutating world. The liberal values of democratic modernism—such as equality, progress and justice—are losing their hold over social processes, from communication to political and economic organization. The molecular components of late modernity are withdrawing from the control of its molar, that is, institutional, political forms. The chemical processes of the social imagination have been so deeply affected that the political model based on consensus and representation tends to lose all meaning and become an ineffective ritual.

Our task here is therefore to study late-modern forms of political power in their interaction with video media. In Italy during these years, videocracy—the late-modern process of neo-authoritarian technopolitical practices—appears in the almost caricatured form of Berlusconi's teledictatorship. But it would be wrong to overemphasize it through a sort of scandalous specificity. What occurred in Italy in the mid-1990s actually represents a process that was already occurring on a global scale: the progressive occupation of the space of social communication by private holdings, and the progressive subordination of political power and the dynamics of democracy to the absolute power of the media-financial complex. Without nostalgia for the old forms of representative democracy, we must analyze the profound mutation that humankind is experiencing in order to seek out a new meaning for the word "democracy," and the new rules by which it functions.

In this book we survey thirty years of sociocultural and political transformations, focusing on the field of Italian media politics. The first half of the book focuses on the Italian teledictatorship, documenting in two chapters Berlusconi's rise to power and his hold on media outlets. Chapter 1 will provide the historical background, while chapter 2 addresses the socioeconomic conditions of Italian media politics and the nature of Berlusconi's regime. In the second half, in three chapters, we explore Italian media activism: in chapter 3 we document the first Italian autonomous free radio station, Radio Alice; in chapter 4 we first address the transformations of the world's social imaginary as a result of new information technologies, and then look at various Italian cases of digital media activism; finally, in chapter 5 we chronicle the experience of OrfeoTV, the first Italian micro-TV station and the bulkhead of the Telestreet network.

What is happening in Italy is not an isolated and unique case, but the most explicit (and almost farcical) example of a global attack upon media democracy. This book seeks not only to document the clash between the telecratic regime and the archipelago of Italian media activism, but also to explore the implications that this case has for understanding the global mutations of media politics. For the problem is not solely one of media access, but also concerns the power relations between the dominant socioeconomic groups and subaltern cognitive labor, as well as the anthropological mutations in the communication field concerning the most basic forms of perception, representation and social imagination. In short, it concerns the tension between the neoliberal social model and the antagonistic tendencies contained in the productive capabilities of the general intellect. It is a struggle whose outcome, we hope to think, is yet to be determined.

one

Berlusconi: The Not-So-Irresistible
Rise of a Media Dictator

On January 26, 1994, the media tycoon Silvio Berlusconi—owner of three private national TV networks, three cable channels, various newspapers and print media sources, as well as businesses in sectors ranging from cinema to advertising, from supermarkets to financial services, including AC Milan, the most famous soccer team in Italy—addressed the nation on all three of his national networks, announcing his decision to enter politics for the good of the country. Wearing a blue cardigan, alone at his desk, with a shelf of books behind him, he delivered an eight-minute speech that started with: "Italy is the country I love." He told the national audience that he had to "take the field," adopting the soccer metaphor to describe his entrance into politics, and asked all Italians to do the same—to take the field to build for themselves and their children a new Italian economic miracle.

Two weeks later, on February 6, 1994, at the first convention of *Forza Italia* [FI, Forward Italy]—another allusion to soccer, invoking the cheer for the national team, i.e., "Go Italy"—on a stage that looked like the creation of a science-fiction writer, with a giant screen behind him, his image surrounded by a blue halo, the biggest entrepreneur of Italian media declared to an ecstatic audience: "Coming here in the car, I thought I was a mad person going to meet other mad people.... You are so many here today.... Our madness is spreading.... The great Erasmus said that true wisdom does not come from reason but from a far-sighted, extraordinary madness." He went on to say that only his crazy altruism had induced him to leave the world of business and dedicate himself to the public's welfare. He had to save Italy from its looming economic crisis and, above all, from the danger of a communist victory.

Berlusconi forgot to mention the fact that his immense holding company, Fininvest, was on the verge of financial breakdown due to the massive debt it had accumulated over the preceding decade. He did not mention that the parties of the center-left—which appeared ready to triumph—were talking openly about passing anti-trust measures that would have forced him to unload one or two of his national networks. He also forgot to mention that Fininvest was under investigation for paying political bribes in connection with the corruption scandal known as *Tangentopoli* [Kickback City], and that his good old friend Bettino Craxi (the socialist former prime minister indicted in 1993 for corruption) could no longer offer him political protection.

Rather than altruism, it was Berlusconi's fear of being prosecuted or forced to declare bankruptcy that prompted him to run for office. Berlusconi launched a campaign that took Italy by storm by combining telegenic charm, can-do entrepreneurial rhetoric and a confident smile. In a three-month televised marathon, Berlusconi brought to power the political alliance that he had founded and directed. In the March 1994 general elections, Forza Italia won the vote of a quarter of the electorate, becoming the party of relative majority. It had attracted most of the constituency that had previously supported the parties involved in the Tangentopoli scandal—the Christian Democracy, the Socialist Party and parts of the lay parties—but this was not enough to hold power. Forza Italia needed allies, and there was no shortage of them. One was the right-wing party *Alleanza Nazionale* [AN, National Alliance], the direct heir of *Movimento Sociale Italiano* [MSI, Italian Social Movement], the party that after World War II collected those nostalgic for the rule of Benito Mussolini. The other ally was the *Lega Nord* [LN, Northern League], led by Umberto Bossi, the expression of social aggressiveness and tax rebellion of the localist classes of Northern Italy, who, though taking advantage of the economic effects of globalization, did not want to accept the social costs of immigration. With these allies, plus a tiny party derived from the remains of the Christian Democrats, Berlusconi occupied the *palazzo di governo* [governor's palace] for several months. It was not a pleasant experience, but at least a short one: in his seven months in power, Berlusconi's problems with the justice system virtually paralyzed the country, and he proved unable to translate into political action anything but his self-interests. His shaky government coalition collapsed because of infightings among his ruling partners after he was indicted for bribery in November 1994.

Though in 1996 the center-left won the special elections (by a narrow margin), Berlusconi became the leading figure of the opposition, biding his time until the next elections while being able to use the political process to gain parliamentary immunity for those business associates who were most vulnerable to arrest for corruption (thus in the best position to implicate him). By 1998 he had been able to refinance his company, renaming it Mediaset, and get new bank loans and sell its shares to outside investors. More importantly, he managed to keep control of 45 percent of the TV audiences and 90 percent of the television advertising market. He used this advantage in the 2001 elections, which he easily won. And with the experience of 1994 under his belt, he set up a much stronger government, this time able to go the distance.

Berlusconi was elected twice, thanks in part to his control of the media landscape, from television stations to newspapers, from polling institutes to advertising agencies. After his second victory in a decade, his rise to the premiership in 2001 paved the way to absolute control over the national media system. For the first time in a Western democracy, the instruments of political, financial and media power were concentrated in the hands of one person. How did this happen? In this chapter we will address this question through a reconstruction of the history of the relationships between political power and the communication system in Italy since World War II.

Media and Power in the Post-War Period: State Monopoly and Clerical Dominance

On telecommunication matters, the Italian legislature has always asserted the state's right to tightly control the media. During Mussolini's fascist regime, the government had given *Ente Italiano Audizioni Radiofoniche* [EIAR, Italian Radio Transmission Corporation] a monopoly over all radio broadcasting in the peninsula. EIAR was a public corporation controlled by the state and accountable to it. In addition, the Fascist Party controlled an agency for broadcasting to rural areas, the *Ente Radio Rurale* [Rural Radio Corporation]. The regime used the evocative qualities of radio sounds for propaganda purposes, mixed with a great deal of classical music, opera and radio dramas. As everywhere in the 1930s, radio was the first medium in Italy to introduce listeners to the sounds and rhythms of industrial society, with its signaling of the hour, music for calisthenics and morning weather report. Surprisingly, it appears that few Italians during that era listened to foreign stations that were easily received at night. Only during the Second World War did Italians begin to listen to Allied transmissions, especially Radio London, to receive information that was censored by the government.

After the war, telecommunications were taken firmly into the hands of the government, which since 1948 had been composed of various coalitions of center-right parties centered on the Christian Democrats. With the introduction of television in 1954, a new state company, *Radiotelevisione Italiana* [RAI, or Italian Broadcasting Corporation], was formed to impose a severe code of conduct on the nascent television industry. From its very beginning, RAI was controlled by the Christian Democrats and heavily influenced by the Catholic Church. RAI regularly offered religious education programs, and news and current affairs programs with a heavily anti-Communist bias. Light music, variety shows, quiz shows and sports events made up the great majority of RAI's broadcasts. As P. Ginsborg noted, attempts to control television's content were particularly evident in the field of advertising: "Forced to choose between America's laissez-faire inundations and the BBC's total ban, RAI came out with a uniquely Italian form of advertising: advertisements were grouped together in a half-hour program called *Carosello* which was transmitted at peak viewing time, just after the eight o'clock news" (Ginsborg 1990: 240).

Carosello formed a first generation of TV viewers by segmenting television time:

shows for the general audience were on until nine o'clock, and afterwards there were shows with adult content. Children were greatly attracted to the narrative character of *Carosello* spots, each lasting 110 seconds. Product names could be mentioned only at the beginning and for five seconds at the end of each spot, leaving the rest of the time to be filled with stories, cartoons and songs. In this seemingly innocuous way, children were introduced to the delights of consumerism. By 1960, three years after its introduction, *Carosello* was the most watched television program in Italy (Calabrese 1975).

By then television had become a mass phenomenon. The 88,000 subscribers of 1954 had grown to one million in 1958. By 1965, 49 percent of Italian families owned a television set (Ginsborg 1990). During all this time, apart from some isolated instances of independent journalism, RAI had functioned as the megaphone of the Christian Democrats, expressing a clerical and conformist culture whose idea of entertainment was proselytizing and whose idea of news was propaganda. Given that RAI was financed by *Istituto per la Ricostruzione Industriale* [IRI, Institute for Industrial Reconstruction]—one of Europe's largest public corporations—its top managers were appointed by the government, namely, the Christian Democrats. With their strategy of occupying all levels of public corporations, the Christian Democrats used RAI as yet another tool for reinforcing their power. Starting in the mid-1950s, key RAI positions, one by one, were filled with party loyalists. Under Ettore Bernabei, protégé of the Christian Democrat leader Amintore Fanfani, RAI was run in a feudal fashion. Not only were RAI's personnel decisions dictated from top to bottom by party affiliation rather than professional qualification, but the entire programming operation was also determined by the Christian Democrats and their allies, thus creating a suffocating and stagnant environment. TV shows, for instance, were not to "bring discredit on or undermine the institution of the family; nor were they to portray attitudes, poses or particulars which might arouse base instincts" (Ginsborg 1990: 240).

The Liberalization of Airwaves and the Birth of the Free Radio Movement: Autonomy and Communication

In the late 1960s, when social movements erupted all over Italy, the world of communication was not immune to the call for change. The need for greater pluralism in newscasts and television programming in general slowly gathered momentum. It was immediately apparent that this need could not be met within the state system of RAI monopoly. This realization produced the first attempts to break the state monopoly through a liberalization of radio and television broadcasting, and by opening the airwaves to private ventures.

It was not until 1974, however, that the broadcasting world saw a significant political change. In that year, the *Corte Costituzionale*, Italy's Supreme Court, declared the state monopoly on airwaves unconstitutional, creating the conditions for independent local broadcasting. In the spring of 1976, the first "free radios" started local operations in various Italian cities. Among them was Radio Alice, a Bolognese radio station that became the loudspeaker of the spontaneous, anti-authoritarian and creative youth movement that exploded in 1977 (see chapter 3). In Milan, Canale 96 started broadcasting, and in Rome, Radio Città Futura. All over Italy, radio ventures were formed, financed and produced by small political collectives, feminist groups, independent journalists, artists, poets, musicians—by people, in short, who could not get access to the public broadcasting service because they were not supported by any powerful politicians. It was a strong explosion, and its effects were clearly felt in the following years. By the end of 1976, 300 radio stations more or less associated with the youth movement formed their own association, the *Federazione Radio Emittenti Democratiche* [FRED, Democratic Radio Broadcasters Federation], based on a clear anti-authoritarian platform. The year 1977 was crucial for Italian society and culture. It marked the emergence of a political identity independent from traditional parties—above all the *Partito Comunista Italiano* [PCI, Italian Communist Party]—among students and young workers. A process of radical cultural secularization also began, as well as a critique of all ideologies that had dominated the national cultural landscape with their moralism and hypocrisy.

Moreover, 1977 saw the birth of a new sociocultural figure destined to have a leading role in the next decade: the semiotic operator, a professional specializing in information, artistic expression, or mass communication techniques. These were mostly young people who had been exposed to the theories and techniques of mass culture and had come to see themselves as producers of communication for a mass market. In this light, we understand how 1977 signals the passage from industrial society (and from the mechanical labor that produced goods through physical effort) to a postindustrial society (in which directly productive intellectual work plays a central role). In this process, intellectual labor—or more precisely, cognitive labor—began to undergo the effects of the alienation of capitalist production.

The youth movement of 1977 developed an innovative awareness of these problems, particularly that economic laws and political power tended to put down intellectual, artistic and techno-scientific activity. This is the reason why their revolt had an originality not found in any other movement of the twentieth century, and why it was geared not only against Western capital but also against the authoritarianism of the communist parties, especially the PCI (who returned the antagonism in kind). The movement of 1977 understood the importance of communication with a clarity unprecedented in earlier political protest movements. The problem of communication was central because it was a movement largely composed of artists, intellectuals and poets who were rebelling against the subalternity to which the capitalist system subjected them. The movement anticipated the tendency that would bring the media system to function as a key control mechanism in terms of politics as well as the reproduction of social and economic power. The Italian Left, led by the PCI, did not approve of the libertarian spirit of this movement and its autonomous aspirations, and turned against it with critical reasoning that bears consideration in the light of Berlusconi's videocratic success. Essentially, the representatives of the Communist Party said: "You kids are taking advantage of the freed-up airwaves to start your own little radio stations, full of energy and democratic goodwill. But beware, tomorrow the big financial groups will move in and occupy the entire field of broadcasting. Liberalization is a double-edged sword and media will end up in the hands of the group with the most money to invest."

Today this warning may appear prophetic, but in hindsight the PCI's strident defense of public broadcasting appears to have been a calculated choice, and at least as ill advised as the movement's naïve approach to liberalization. It was a conservative choice, for a politics of the defense of the public system against liberalization was destined to fail. The state monopoly was bound to be defeated, and it was a question of accepting the battle on the terrain of *communication* from below. The people initially associated with the free radio stations fought to carve out a niche in broadcasting, and in the process explored new forms of communication that provided precious opportunities for change.

The Left, especially the PCI, reacted to the social movements of the 1970s with hostility, seeing them as a danger to the unity of the working class and an anarchistic provocation against the state. In those years, PCI policy was defined by the historic compromise of a cultural, and then political, alliance between the forces of the Left and the Catholic forces represented by the Christian Democracy. This alliance reinforced the most conservative components of both parties, such as their fundamentalism and intolerance of unorthodox social behaviors, which were stigmatized as antinational and elitist. The result of this policy was the creation of a system of unified power, closed to every form of social opposition and autonomous cultural expression. This led to a partition of political power that came to be called "consociativism," meaning the sharing of institutional power as well as the economic privileges associated with the spoils system of state patronage. Naturally, the public broadcasting service was affected by consociativism, and it became a sort of cultural manifestation of the conformism of the party-centric regime. Instead of engaging itself in the liberalization of broadcasting, or supporting local initiatives in the communication domain, the Left asked for a slice of RAI's monopoly. Their wish was granted. Parliament passed a law reforming the television service under which RAI was divided into three networks according to the political parties: RAI One, the most-established and best-financed network, remained under the control of the Christian Democrats, and two new networks were created to accommodate the socialists and the PCI, who received RAI Two and RAI Three respectively. In this way, the state monopoly tried to resist the liberalization process initiated by the *Corte Costituzionale* in its 1975 ruling and put into effect by the free radio stations, but it was eventually abused by private television networks. The Left completely underestimated the importance of the liberalization of the broadcasting system. Pursuing a logic of state patronage and clientelism, of consociativism and political harmony, the Left distanced itself from the capillary process of spontaneous and autonomous communicative production initiated by the free radio stations.

The year 1977 was pivotal in the history of politics and communication in Italy. It marked a moment of passage from the modernist scenario of the twentieth century—with its conflicts between clearly recognizable classes, its ambitious ideological prospects, and its industrial production system—to the postmodern scenario in which ideological conflicts attenuate, human activity increasingly shifts toward immaterial production, labor becomes intellectualized, and politics becomes a televised spectacle.

In Italy, much more than anywhere else, 1977 was marked by the explosion of movements that rejuvenated the cultural and political patrimony of previous social movements—above all, the 1968 era of collective action—and foreshadowed the postindustrial transition. Unfortunately, these movements did not succeed in constructing an autonomous communication system, partly because the parties of the Left remained mired in their antiquated political logic, and reduced these movements to marginal elements from which they drew energy to consolidate their own power. The Left was unprepared to affront the neoliberal ideologues that took control of Western economic policies in the 1980s.

During these years, newly formed corporations absorbed the energies of that movement by co-opting its most capable members with entrepreneurial opportunities and promises of great financial rewards. This was particularly clear in the arena of media production. Journalists who developed their skills in the free radio movement were made into media professionals by commercial networks; artists who had expressed their rebellious creativity on city walls were hired by Milan's advertisement agencies; poets became copywriters; and so on. In short, the social intelligence and technical competence of the social movements of 1977 were bought by private entrepreneurs who were organizing the assault on the collective imaginary.

The movement of autonomous communication had the communicative competence but lacked the financial means to create an independent production circuit. In Italy, only the political parties, through the welfare services of the local governments, could have played such a role, but their hostility toward the spontaneous movements made such a collaboration impossible. The result was that the people from these movements were seduced by the financial means of big business and, from these creative experiments, Berlusconi was able to draw the blood that nourished his media monster.

From Liberalization to Duopoly: Berlusconi and his Twin Brother

The formation of Berlusconi's media empire started in 1974 with Telemilano Cavo, a local cable-TV station broadcasting neighborhood council meetings, information on available services, and the occasional movie for the tenants of Milano 2, a 700,000 square-meter residential complex built entirely by Berlusconi in Milan's suburbs (Berlusconi had convinced some local politicians to reroute the flight patterns of a Milan airport, turning a noisy and unattractive piece of real estate into a financial goldmine). Four year later, Telemilano started broadcasting to the entire city of Milan from a studio built in the storeroom of the Jolly Hotel in Milano 2. Berlusconi's channel, which took the name *Canale 5* [Channel 5], was able to lure media personalities away from RAI, including Mike Bongiorno, the most popular quiz-show host on Italian television. It succeeded in acquiring movies never before shown on television (such as the library of Titanus International), and it also broadcast American television series (such as Dallas). It was around this latter type of transmission that the audience of Canale 5 was built, as well as the culture and imaginary that emerged in the 1980s, with their particular mix of cynicism, aggressive hedonism and opportunism.

In the years following 1977, everyday life changed dramatically. The social engagement and playful practices of the youth movement were replaced by political terrorism, drug abuse, the retreat into private life and the abandonment of collective action. The gathering places of the collectives, the youth centers, were squashed by police repression, attacked by aggressive magistrates, and undermined by the infiltration of heavy drugs and the seduction of armed struggle. The autonomy movement gradually disappeared, and in its place emerged armed and violent groups such as the *Brigate Rosse* [Red Brigades] and *Prima Linea* [First Line].

The cities themselves changed shape: people abandoned the streets and piazzas and stayed home in the evening. The urban landscape evoked fear and sadness. Social anxiety spread with heroin abuse. Berlusconi's television fed into this melancholization of the urban environment: *"Torna a casa in tutta fretta c'è Canale 5 che ti aspetta"* [Hurry, hurry home, channel 5 is waiting for you] was one slogan of the new television network launched by the enterprising Milanese lawyer. Depressing, yes, but also accurate and appealing.

In 1979, Berlusconi founded Fininvest to control his growing interest in the media business. A year later, Canale 5 became a national network. It circumvented the law reserving the national airwaves for RAI by buying numerous small, regional stations, and by having each one broadcast the same program just seconds apart, thus achieving a national audience (and high ad rates) while appearing to obey the letter of the law. In 1981, Berlusconi founded Publitalia, an advertising holding company that in few years gained control of 80 percent of the national business. In 1982, he bought another network, Italia 1, owned by the publisher Edilio Rusconi. In that same year he bought the television company Telealtomilanese (owned by the Rizzoli family) and its extensive film library, which included the best of Italian neorealism, for next to nothing. The Rizzoli man who offered Berlusconi such a sweet inside deal, Enzo Scognamiglio, found himself on the ballot for Forza Italia in 1994 and was elected to the Senate—of which he became the president. In 1984, Berlusconi acquired his final national network based on local distribution, *Retequattro* [Channel 4], from Mondadori. Belusconi managed all the deals and the operations of the networks, down to the minutest detail. The Italian journalist Enzo Biagi bitterly commented: "If Berlusconi had tits, he would also play the co-hostess on his network's game shows."

The ideological and communicative style that we associate with Berlusconi was shaped during these years. While Italian society was overwhelmed by anxiety, fear and depression, and while the Left insisted on imposing sacrifices upon the working class in order to curb inflation and lift the country out of the recession, a new sociopolitical configuration emerged based on superficial optimism and competitive individualism. This configuration found its political expression in the new secretary of the Socialist Party, Bettino Craxi, and its sociocultural definition in Berlusconi's media. The prospect of liberalization and democratization expressed by the movement of 1977 was twisted into a process of cultural transformation in which intellectual labor was engulfed by the economic cycle of corruption. After Tangentopoli, Craxi was vilified for many years, up until his death in exile in 2000; however, we cannot forget that it was Craxism that accomplished the secularization of Italian society and its partial emancipation from the two dominant churches of those years: the Catholic church of the Pope, De Gasperi and Andreotti, and the Communist church of Togliatti, Longo and Berlinguer.

Above all, Craxism followed the transformation of Italian society, centering it on immaterial production, entertainment and show business. Craxi, and later Berlusconi, were the leaders of a new social class, a type of *lumpenbourgeoisie* that profited from the economic transition from an organic industrial system to a polymorphous infoproduction system.

This class became wealthy through the growth of imaginary commodities: advertising, financial services (especially speculative financing), and the global cycle of information and entertainment. The power of the lumpenbourgeoisie was founded upon the libertarian attacks on state monopolies of the 1970s. But while the Left was busily defending the public monopoly on information instead of supporting the democratic proliferation of broadcasting centers, Craxi and Berlusconi took advantage of the breakup of the monopoly and little by little managed to control the entire domain of national media.

During the 1980s, as Craxi's political and Berlusconi's cultural leadership solidified, Italian society became increasingly secularized, freeing itself from the dogmas of both the Christian Democrats and the Communists. However, the lumpenbourgeoisie was in turn producing its own dogma, no less powerful than former ones, of financial success through greed and aggressiveness. And this ideology was the center of the winning class values of the yuppie years.

Both Craxi and Berlusconi were marked by the same aggressive optimism— the belief in efficiency, the mirage of financial success, ruthless competition and hyperactivism. Their optimism dominated the Italian sociopolitical landscape of the 1980s, but this optimism had a macabre side, consisting of a mishmash of vulgar jokes, squalid stripteases, sexual blackmail, hypocrisy and existential poverty. It was the optimism of bad taste, of success at the expense of the weak, and organized societal plundering.

Craxi's political actions were indissoluble from Berlusconi's television and advertising policy. For fifteen years they shared their activities in perfect harmony. For fifteen years they marched to the same tune of national recovery written by the secret Masonic Lodge P2 (to which they both belonged). For fifteen years they locked people in their homes to watch billions of hours of television, while boasting that this was the best of all possible worlds.

During this period, Berlusconi produced the psychochemical social conditions for Craxi's political success while Craxi created the political conditions for the ultimate conquest of the Italian infosphere by his good friend Berlusconi. During his entire political tenure, Craxi—leader of the PSI for fifteen straight years and Italy's prime minister for four—supported the formation of Berlusconi's empire by contempt of Italian laws, public opinion and good taste.

The first legal case was brought against Berlusconi in 1984. As we have seen, the national broadcasting of Canale 5 was in violation of the law. For years this violation was tolerated by the silent complicity of Parliament. On October 16, 1984, acting on the protest of a small cartel of independent television stations, three local magistrates ordered the blackout of Canale 5 within the territory under their jurisdiction. Craxi, then prime minister, responded swiftly. He invited Berlusconi to Parliament, and immediately declared the magistrate's action void through a legal decree tailored to his friend's needs. Canale 5 continued its broadcasts. This would not be the last time Craxi intervened on Berlusconi's behalf. Berlusconi thanked his friend in several ways. He made Craxi the best man at his wedding to his second wife, and prosecutors in Milan later located at least $6 million that was moved from foreign bank accounts belonging to Fininvest to bank accounts in Tunisia they believed were controlled by Craxi.

In those years, Berlusconi also began to buy print media. First he bought *Sorrisi e Canzoni*, a weekly magazine that he transformed into a TV guide for his networks. Then he bought *Il Giornale Nuovo*, a daily Milanese newspaper directed by Indro Montanelli, and lastly he launched an assault against the editorial giant Mondadori, owner of the most read Italian daily newspaper, *Il Giornale Nuovo*, and two political weeklies, *L'Espresso* and *Panorama*. His takeover was contested by another mogul, Carlo De Benedetti, chief executive officer of Olivetti, an Italian computer company, who had joined forces with Fiat, the biggest Italian carmaker, in his attempt to wrestle control of Mondadori. After a hard-fought battle the matter went to arbitration, and the judge responsible for the decision, Vittorio Metta (at the time, judge of the Civil Appellate Court in Rome), ruled that Berlusconi should be awarded all of Mondadori's holdings, with the exception of *Il Giornale Nuovo* and *L'Espresso*.

In the following years, judicial investigations revealed that the judgment regarding the ownership of Mondadori had been heavily influenced by Berlusconi's lawyers, especially by Cesare Previti. The lawyers had bribed the presiding magistrates in order to obtain a favorable judgment. After this highly suspect and contested victory, several sectors of public opinion began to sound an alarm regarding the increasing power of Fininvest within the national mediascape. It was time to regulate the jungle. Thanks to Craxi, the regulation became a pure and simple legitimization of the accumulated power of Berlusconi.

In 1990, a new law on media ownership (called the *Legge Mammì* [Mammì Law], after the name of its main proponent) was drafted by the Craxi-controlled government. The Mammì Law stated that any private corporation could own up to three national networks. At this point, Berlusconi owned three paid cable channels. The new law allowed any private corporation to own up to three paid cable channels and it contained two measures that created the appearance of sacrifice on Berlusconi's part. One forced him to give up most of his share of a pay-TV satellite network, while the other established that the owner of a national TV network could not also possess a national daily newspaper. Berlusconi got around the second by "selling" his daily newspaper, the conservative *Il Giornale*, to his brother, Paolo. (He sold off most of his stock in the satellite-TV venture to a group of investors, some of whom he actually lent money, thereby enabling them to make the purchase.)

But the real scandal of the Mammì Law was that Berlusconi's company Fininvest had paid off the principal drafters of the legislation. In 1993, a government official acknowledged receiving a 10 billion lire bribe (approximately $8 million at the time) for Minister Mammì and his party. Mammì's legislative aide, David Giacolone, received a personal payment of more than $300,000—which Fininvest insists was a "consulting fee," but which magistrates considered a bribe.

The Berlusconi-Craxi tandem control of Italian society continued to prosper until a group of Milanese prosecutors (known thereafter as the *Mani Pulite* [Clean Hands Team]) began to prosecute the widespread corruption in the economic and government arenas. Led by the prosecutor Antonio de Pietro, within a few years Tangentopoli unveiled corruption at the highest levels of government, from the Socialist ex-prime minister Craxi to the Christian Democrat ex-prime minister and senator-for-life Andreotti, as well as a within number of business institutions (including, for example the Enimont corporation). By 1993, hundreds of politicians were under investigation—virtually the entire regime of the 1980s was going to jail. By 1994, Berlusconi was wiped out of political allies: Craxi had fled the country after having been indicted on too many counts of corruption, the Socialist Party was in disarray, and Andreotti had been disgraced. When he decided to run for political office, Berlusconi portrayed himself as a businessman without political connections, an enemy of political clientelism. Nothing could have been further from the truth. Berlusconi, since the very beginning of his career, had been helped and protected by the Mafia-like political cartel, and by the highest state offices throughout the 1980s. The last years of the CAF alliance (named after Craxi, Andreotti and Forlani—who, like Andreotti, was another leader of the Christian Democrats, and was also found guilty of having accepted tens of millions of dollars in kickbacks) were years of strict symbiosis with Fininvest's media power. The Fininvest empire manufactured ideologies and dominance strategies for the CAF alliance, providing it with the support of its millions of viewers. In return, CAF paved the road for private media penetration and occupation of the social imaginary. Orwell's dystopic imagination seems to have found in Italy its first realization precisely in 1984, the year that Craxi legalized the practices of the emerging company. Media saturation of reality and the progressive political barbarization of everyday life had finally found each other.

By 1994, when Berlusconi decided to enter politics, prosecutors had begun to discover the trail of Fininvest bribes, and Berlusconi's political protectors were either in jail, under indictment or had fled the country. "If I don't enter politics, they'll tear me to pieces," he told Indro Montanelli, the editor-in-chief of *Il Giornale*. Montanelli was to become one of the first victims of the conflicts of interest created by the new hybrid creature, Berlusconi-politician. Sharing a basic conservative orientation with Montanelli, Berlusconi had left him free to run the newspaper, which Montanelli himself founded. But when *Il Giornale* refused to endorse Berlusconi as a candidate, Montanelli found himself under siege. First there were angry calls from Berlusconi himself—even though he had officially sold the paper to his brother. Then the anchorman of one of Berlusconi's TV networks actually called for Montanelli's resignation on the air. Finally, Berlusconi entered the newsroom and insisted on addressing the staff himself, berating them for their fainthearted support. Montanelli resigned in protest after the incident and a more pliant editor was hired.

In his campaign for the election, Berlusconi showed how powerful the synergy of media and politics could be. His campaign manager, Marcello Dell'Utri, was the head of the advertising wing of Fininvest, a company called Pubblitalia. Dell'Utri used the sales staff of the company as his electoral machine and recruited a vast number of candidates from among Berlusconi employees, consultants and business partners. Forza Italia became known as the *partito-azienda* [company party].

Berlusconi introduced a new level of media sophistication into Italian political life. He blanketed the airwaves with catchy, slickly produced commercials and was constantly present on every network. Moreover, the Fininvest news broadcasts were virtually indistinguishable from advertisements. When handling the delicate issue of political bribery, Berlusconi's news broadcasters would actually read company press releases as if they were independently prepared newscasts (a practice later rediscovered by the Bush II propaganda machine).

From the Private-Public Duopoly to Berlusconi's Monopoly

1994, the year of the transition from the First to the Second Republic, was marked by the general election on March 27, 1994. For the first time in Italian history, an election was based on a majoritarian, winner-take-all system, as opposed to the proportional system used since 1945.

Berlusconi's Forza Italia, and its allies from the Right, easily won the election. Berlusconi's most faithful ally was the neo-fascist Alleanza Nazionale, which won 14 percent of the vote and its first chance in almost 50 years to be part of a government. The second ally was the Lega Nord, which ran a federalist platform based on Northern Italy's pride in its self-disciplined and hard-working people, while attacking Rome and the South for their corruption and patronage. The Lega Nord was in the frontline of the struggle against the corruption of the old regime, which they accused of being anti-Northern and "too Roman." Although the Lega Nord only got 8 percent of the vote, due to the geographic concentration of their support, they were able to translate this small portion into a great number of seats in Parliament. Since the Lega Nord strongly supported the judiciary's indictments against the leaders of the previous regime, its alliance with Berlusconi and the many "recycled" politicians who had found a place in Forza Italia produced some uneasiness and augured a difficult cohabitation. Finally, there was a third ally: the *Centro Cristiano Democratico* [CCD, Christian Democratic Center], the remains of the right wing of the old Christian Democrats. They were Catholic fundamentalists, fervent pro-lifers and entrenched politicians commanding the Southern vote, including that of organized crime. Their six percent of the vote guaranteed them a minor role in new cabinet.

In April 1994, this motley crew assumed the power democratically granted by the Italian voters. From the very beginning it was crystal clear that one of their prime targets for control was the communications field. The "new" regime wanted to seize control of RAI, where the Left still had some influence. One of the first acts of Berlusconi's government was indeed an attack on RAI, which it claimed was poorly managed and too costly. Notwithstanding the obvious conflict of interest, Berlusconi proposed that government support of RAI be eliminated. Of course the government did not mention that there was a conflict of interest, though in less-guarded moments, Berlusconi remarked that he saw no reason for his government to financially support his political opposition. With the pure and simple elimination of RAI, Berlusconi would have been able to enjoy complete control over the Italian airwaves, but this suggestion caused a firestorm, and the President of the Republic, Oscar Luigi Scalfaro, intervened. In the end, following a well-established Italian strategy, a compromise was reached. RAI was allowed to survive, but in exchange Berlusconi was allowed to remove RAI's board of directors and replace the news directors of all three state networks with pro-Berlusconi people, in some cases his former employees. The Lega Nord gave him a hard time in the nomination process of the new board of directors, but eventually acquiesced.

Thus, Berlusconi had 90 percent of Italy's TV airwaves at his disposal. He became the sole agent of telecommunication. But then things began to go wrong.

In June 1994, the World Cup soccer final between Italy and Brazil went into overtime, and penalty kicks were needed to decide the winner. AC Milan's forward Daniele Massaro, a Forza Italia sympathizer who only a week before had declared that losing to Nigeria would have been a national shame, missed the decisive kick, and sent the entire Italian population into a general depression. Berlusconi had been hoping for a victory, and had planned to release, in the week of the celebrations, a government decree of amnesty for many politicians arrested during the corruption investigation. The obvious hope was that the cries of triumph would have covered the cries in opposition to this amnesty. But in the absence of that victory, when Berlusconi decree's came into effect—with the result that many of the politicians arrested in Operation Clean Hands were released from jail overnight—the response of the Italian population registered loud and clear: corrupt politicians had to be tried, and the "Save the Thieves Decree" (as it came to be known) was withdrawn. After that, Berlusconi's lucky star faded quickly. When the government attempted to attack the pension system, social opposition became so strong that in the end, the Lega Nord withdrew its support of the government and provoked the fall of Berlusconi's government. His first political era was over.

Five Years of the Center-Left

In 1995, after the fall of the first Berlusconi government, a year-long confused period followed during which Lamberto Dini, a man who had initially supported Berlusconi and then distanced himself from him, led a transition government propped up by the center-left parties.

Lamberto Dini was a trusted man of international finance, and made the passage from the rambling populism of the center-right coalition to a modernist version of liberalism possible, from which center-left government, in its various incarnations, was interpreted over the following years. General elections were held again in April 1996. In the meantime, the forces of the center-left—in particular the *Democratici di Sinistra* [DS, Democrats of the Left], the main party of the Left founded in 1991 after reshaping the PCI into a moderate-left political party and the *Democrazia è Libertà – La Margherita* [DL, Democracy is Freedom] or "Daisy," a smaller party which combined liberal parties with centrist former-Christian Democrats—had agreed on the nomination of a centrist, Romano Prodi, and formed a "progressive" coalition for the upcoming elections.

A Professor of Economics at the University of Bologna, Prodi had been a representative of the Christian Democracy, and in the past had directed the IRI, an institute that brought together state-run companies. His position had always been far from the unchained liberalism of the center-right, and a very broad democratic array assembled around his figure—ranging from the Christian Left to the wide area of the former communists. The "progressives" won the election and formed a government backed by a coalition that took the name *Ulivo* [Olive Tree], and was supported from the outside by *Partito di Rifondazione Comunista* [PRC, Communist Refoundation], a party founded in 1991 that brought together nostalgics from the old Communist Party with a somewhat heterogeneous formation of Trotskyites and grassroots trade union organizations.

Prodi's political program represented the refusal of the ideological fanaticism of the Right, but his political appeal depended on two features: the construction of an original media scenario and his European credentials. Berlusconi had built his image on the aggressiveness of the victorious social classes, on their exasperation with the cadences of political polemic, on the legitimatization of old nationalist myths now proposed through the soccer imaginary, and on an unscrupulous and spectacular modernism. Prodi was the perfect character to spoil this game.

Prodi is from Emilia, a region of north-central Italy which during the century-long process of modernization had managed to balance urban industrial development with community values, keep the focus of its cities on the local inhabitants, and sustain an efficient public administration (especially in local services, from housing to education to health care). Furthermore, Prodi knew how to transfer his Emilian good nature to a media image: his regional Italian recalled that of Emilian peasants, his quiet and preachy delivery had the cadenza of a rural priest, his plump face inspired avuncular trust and earned him the nickname "*mortadella*" (a type of Emilian cold-cut ham, like bologna). Berlusconi—the Milanese businessman who promised a million new jobs but didn't deliver any—couldn't survive the comparison with the Emilian economics professor. The televised clashes between Berlusconi and Prodi turned into a defeat of the image of the man who had built his power on image. To Berlusconi's optimistic and high-sounding declarations, Prodi responded with calm, returning a tenor of realism that reassured viewers.

On a political level, Prodi's trump card, and that of the center-left coalition he represented, was his relationship with European institutions, especially the decision-making centers of the European Union. Berlusconi has never been well regarded by the crucial countries of the European Union. Particularly in France, public opinion and high state officials starting with then-President Mitterand, regarded Forza Italia and Berlusconi as a dangerous eruption of anti-democratic populism. The European Economic Authority, which in those years was putting the finishing touches on the common monetary system in preparation for the launch of the single currency, did not demonstrate much confidence in the choices of the Italian government. Prodi was clearly better prepared to keep the country plugged in to Europe not only in economic terms, but above all in cultural terms.

In 1996, Berlusconi entrusted his image to the immaterial level of electronic media, especially during news broadcasts, going as far as to have Emilio Fede, the most faithful of his networks' news anchormen, declare that he would leave the country if the "communists" won the elections. Prodi, on the other hand, launched a campaign of imaginary reterritorialization. He rented a bus, and for forty days he traveled the length and breadth of Italy, organizing meetings in the different regions, establishing a dialogue with an audience of professionals, workers and students everywhere he went. Prodi's European credentials combined with his down-to-earth media appeal proved the difference, and the center-left coalition won the elections by a narrow margin.

In a certain sense, Prodi's victory represented the refusal of a certain technomedia determinism, according to which domination over the television system automatically translates into winning the consensus of the majority. But that is not the case. Certainly, communication technologies put powerful devices in the hands of political power, but this means that politics must assimilate the language of the media—it must play that game. And this is what Romano Prodi succeeded in doing. The bus played counterpoint to the television on the level of the imaginary.

Prodi's government was backed by a diverse and divided center-left coalition, and had to rely on the external support of the PRC in order to govern. Thus it was based on a fragile equilibrium, which ruptured after two years of government. In 1998, the PCR demanded, as a condition for their continued support, a radical social policy—in particular the reduction of the working week to thirty-five hours. It was an attempt to remove Italy from the orbit of liberalist politics that had dominated the decade. Moderate elements of the center-left certainly had no intention of making such a break with international liberalism. The frame of reference for the Italian center-left was the Third Way of Blair and Clinton, not the pluralist Left of French prime minister Lionel Jospin, who during those years tried (with little luck) to launch a social policy based on the reduction of the working week to thirty-five hours. The center-left could not accept the PCR's ultimatum, and so, after lengthy negotiations and a confidence vote in Parliament lost by three votes, Prodi decided to resign.

The center-left was faced with a choice: call a new election, or try to form a new government. Many on the Left thought that it would be better to go to the polls straight away, and seek a new mandate for a center-left government. Ultimately,

however, the second option prevailed. Massimo D'Alema, secretary of the Left Democrats, the party which had picked up the majority of the old communist electorate,
managed to obtain the backing of the same forces that had previously supported
Prodi. But in the meantime, suspicions and rivalries had weakened the center-left
block. Prodi's supporters felt doubly betrayed at the hands of the former communists. The Olive Tree, the progressive coalition, had lost its unity, and D'Alema did
not have the same type of quiet authority as Romano Prodi. D'Alema is a man
shaped by late-communist culture, and had made a career as a political functionary
during the 1970s and '80s. After 1989, like many Communist Party functionaries
of the Brezhnev era, D'Alema refashioned himself as a reformist. The definition of
"reformist" lost its original connotations during the 1990s. The reformism of the
former communists in Russia, as in Italy and elsewhere, is above all the mark of a
cultural supplication to liberal ideology. While Prodi aroused mild feelings of ap-
proval throughout the center and the center-left, D'Alema stirred strong feelings of
hostility both in the Catholic milieus close to Prodi and among the radical Left, who
accused him of subalternity to neoliberalism.

Furthermore, D'Alema had to handle the international crisis in the Balkans, in
particular the military intervention in Kosovo against the Serbian Republic. For the
first time since 1945, Italy took part in direct military operations under the aegis
of NATO. The humanitarian motivation for the conflict was not enough to sway
the majority of opinion on the Left. Article 11 of the Constitution states that "Italy
repudiates war as an instrument for the resolution of international conflicts," and
for the vast majority of leftist militants, whether of a Catholic or a Marxist conviction, this violation of a constitutional taboo was an unforgivable offense. D'Alema's
image became distasteful to a large section of the leftist electorate. D'Alema had not
come to government as a result of a direct vote, the electorate had voted for Prodi;
only through political maneuvering had the premiership passed on to him.

In such a weak condition, D'Alema's government could not act on the most press-
ing issue in media politics: re-establishing democratic rules in the field of the media, namely devising a law to dismantle Berlusconi's monopoly. Although they were
leaders of antagonistic groups during those years, D'Alema and Berlusconi behaved
as if they had some sort of under-the-table deal between them. Already in 1996,
shortly after Prodi's victory, D'Alema and Berlusconi had started negotiations for
institutional reforms, establishing a commission for constitutional reform. In the
end nothing came of it and the commission was dissolved, but Berlusconi came out a
winner: the ongoing institutional negotiations had given him credibility as a political
figure, and during the entire period of the negotiations, the attention given to this
initiative impeded a clear policy of condemnation and containment of Berlusconi's
media and economic strategies. This inaction continued even after the failure of the
institutional reforms. Many people had asked D'Alema's government to draw up a
law to establish a maximum limit on media concentration, but it didn't do a thing.
As if paralyzed, the center-left waited for Berlusconi's media machine to regain the
upper hand. This occurred in the spring of 2000, when local elections were held.
They were a disaster for the center-left, and thus foretold an inevitable victory for

the center-right in the next general election, set for the spring of 2001.

The final year of the D'Alema government was agony, not only on the level of policy initiatives, but especially on the level of image. Although judges were collecting evidence of the crimes committed by Berlusconi and his accomplices during this period, and despite the fact that the public expected a legal solution to the conflict of interests, the center-left government did nothing about it.

The boss of the Italian mediascape, left undisturbed during those years of center-left government, threw an enormous amount of resources into the most invasive electoral campaign imaginable. Huge billboards presented Silvio Berlusconi as the workers' president, and as the entrepreneurs' president. In the atria of train stations all over Italy, giant images of Berlusconi and propaganda pavilions were erected. Mediaset spread the views of its political boss daily with news of violence provoked by Moroccan and Albanian barbarians who were arriving in Italy due to the Left's permissiveness. And at RAI, Berlusconi could count on the support of some key anchormen who, preparing themselves for the new change of regime, literally gave him carte blanche. In 2001, Bruno Vespa, host of a program titled *Porta a Porta* [Door to Door], a man who has always distinguished himself by his obsequiousness to political power of any stripe, invited Berlusconi onto his program. Berlusconi capitalized on the fact that *Porta a Porta* aired at prime time and enjoyed high ratings, and chose that forum to perform the signing of 'a contract with Italy.' He turned up with a piece of paper stating his political promises: work for everyone, reduced taxes and huge public works. The program was thoroughly marked by the neoliberal optimism of the 1990s. It was too late, because the times were changing, and the global economy had already entered a phase of recession. But in spring 2001, Berlusconi reinvigorated the illusion by signing his contract with the Italian people on the air.

Quite predictably, Berlusconi succeeded: Forza Italia won a strong majority of seats in Parliament and he formed a ruling coalition, again with Alleanza Nazionale and a much weaker Lega Nord. This time he had every intention to last the full term. Even if his promises had revealed themselves to be unattainable lies, he had nevertheless managed to transform the Italian sociopolitical and media landscape for good.

As expected, the center-right quickly took possession of all C3 levels (communication-command-control) and completely occupied the mediascape, in particular the television system. After winning the 2001 elections, Berlusconi got his hands on what was left of RAI, the state television system. By fall 2001, more than 90 percent of Italian television stations were under the control of people directly answerable to Berlusconi.

The Integrated Communicative System (The Gasparri Law)

The culmination of this transformation and occupation of the mediascape was reached with the Gasparri Law, approved by the Italian parliament in April 2004 (after six tries and the refusal of the President of the Republic to sign an earlier version into law). This reform had as its objective the communicative system and the solution of conflicts of interest that Berlusconi brought with him. It was designed to respond to the widespread sentiment of unease that derived from the domination of the Mediaset group in the panorama of Italian communications. The previous law stated that one of the three television networks owned by Mediaset (Retequattro) could not continue to be broadcast over the airwaves, and had to be transferred to satellite, because one company was not allowed to possess more than two national networks broadcasting analogically. The Gasparri Law provided for the increase of the total amount of television ownership allowed to a private company by enormously widening the terms included in what the law defined as an "integrated communicative system." Mediaset was thus able to continue to broadcast its three national networks. Furthermore, the owners of television networks were also allowed to acquire daily newspapers—something the previous law prohibited (even if Berlusconi always skirted this prohibition by having it appear that his brother or his wife owned the newspapers that the law prevented him from being the titular head of), and were free to invest in "terrestrial" digital broadcasting, a new technology which did not require a satellite dish or cable for the reception of digital programs but just a regular antenna and a decoder box.

The essential picklock to consolidate his empire over the communications system consisted however in the distribution of advertising. RAI and print media were obviously at a disadvantage on this point, and the commercial television networks were awarded the possibility to surpass any existing limit of advertising programming. Infomercials were legalized without limitations, benefiting only the Mediaset empire. The law crystallized the existing divide in the advertising market, in which Mediaset had a 38.3 percent share in 2002. With a similar preeminence, the market leader was able to lower his prices to the detriment of all the others, greatly reducing the slice of the pie available to the rest of print media.

But the legislative masterpiece was the regulation established by the Gasparri Law concerning this problem of the conflict of interest. According to the law, a conflict of interest occurred when "the holder of government responsibilities" participated, proposed or performed actions that had "a specific and preferential impact on the patrimony of the holder, his/her spouse, or relatives up to the second degree, with damage to the public good." Thus it was not ownership that constituted the precedent for a conflict of interest, but management. The "mere owner" was not involved in the interest of his company, and only he who (formally) managed it should be forbidden from making political decisions that could directly concern that company. In this manner Berlusconi was safe. He was only the owner of innumerable communication companies: advertising, television, editorial as well as insurance companies, and so on. And what importance does the owner ever have?

The formulation of the regulation regarding conflict of interest allowed Berlusconi to maintain ownership of his television companies and to preside over a government that regulates and supervises the television system. When matters that directly regarded his interests needed to be discussed, it was enough that Berlusconi graciously absented himself from the floor of the Parliament. He was absent, even though he still remained the head of the government.

Wasn't this an extraordinary exhibition of arrogance, derision and insolence? Of course it was, but it didn't help much to decry these outrages as if they were anomalies to be remedied. "I hold the scepter that allows me to do anything, and thus I will do anything," Jarry's Ubu Rex continually declared. So did Berlusconi: excess was his method and his strength.

Mediascape, the Social Imaginary and Democracy

After Berlusconi's victories in 1994 and 2001, the center-left complained that Berlusconi had used his media interests to win the election. Some political commentators responded that, all in all, the balance between RAI and Fininvest guaranteed equal access, and that the center-left held control of the majority of print media. But such claims are nonsense. During every electoral campaign since 1994, the center-left front had insisted on the need for media fairness. The Parliament even elected a guarantor to monitor equal distribution of airtime among candidates. This claim was also nonsense.

Indeed, Berlusconi's campaign did not start in January 1994, with his acceptance speech full of advertising rhetoric. Rather, Berlusconi had initiated his campaign fifteen years before, when he began to create the psychological, emotional, moral and ideological conditions for the final offensive. Berlusconi had actually begun the first mass campaign to affirm a culture of corruption and arrogance in 1979, when he imported the serial *Dallas* and its character J.R. Forza Italia's 1994 electoral campaign, with its sappy tones and its jingles, was only the finishing touch in that transformation of social attitudes and tastes orchestrated in the preceding decade.

When Berlusconi's final offensive hit, the forces of the center-left did not really understand what was happening. In the 1980s, they had downplayed the political meaning of the creation of a media empire, limiting themselves to the defense of public television and its partitioning among the political parties. As late as 1993, Walter Veltroni, a leading member of the Left Democrats (formerly the PCI) and director of the leftist newspaper *L'Unità*, declared that Berlusconi should be considered, after all, a progressive.

What escaped the center-left was the fact that media power is not defined by its political statements. Television is not a medium for the creation of consensus or for a kind of rational persuasion. It is not a medium that serves to counterbalance logical argument. Television is a means of pervasion, rather than persuasion. It operates on the cognitive modalities for reception, interpretation and decision, rather than on the ideological content of the message. This is why the media populism of Berlusconi won in 1994 and again in 2001, after five years of center-left government.

Why didn't the center-left government make a law regulating the media system and the problem of the conflict of interest? The reason lies in its cultural inability to face the new reality of late-modern society. The old-fashioned culture of the Left has never really grasped the meaning of the emerging mediascape, nor understood the new relationship between media and political power, which has less to do with ideology and content and than it has to do with the systematic and pervasive occupation of people's mental time, subconscious habits, attention and imagination.

In the end, Prime Minister Berlusconi has become the master of the entire Italian media world. In this sense, we can say that an authoritarian system exists in Italy. Its methods are not those of brute force, even if the violent face of the regime has manifested itself—for example, in the Genova repression of protesters during the G8 meeting in July of 2001. Above all else, its method consists of the manipulations of the expectations and the imaginary of the Italian people.

This is the irony of recent Italian history: the same man who started his media empire thanks to social reform and the breakup of the state monopoly caused by media activism has ended up the owner of a new monopolist system. The very conditions of democracy have been severed, not formally, but nonetheless in substance. The most substantive level of democracy, the constitution and functioning of the social imagination, has been corrupted. The most basic freedom, the freedom of thought, has been declared obsolete.

A superficial analysis could conclude that Italy is being thrown back into fascism, with the reemergence of the ideologies and behaviors of Mussolini's regime. But this would be a mistaken interpretation of events. We are not witnessing a comeback of past ideologies. What we are confronting is the power of broadcasting electronic nothingness out of the vacuum of the cathode ray tube.

Etymologically speaking, the word "fascism" comes from the bundle (or fasces) of rods bound about an axe with a projecting blade, carried by ancient Roman magistrates as a symbol of their authority. Mussolini took this image to symbolize the strength derived from people's willingness to be bound together in what he called *fasci di combattimento* [combat fasces].

In the integrated system of communication, the videocracy is represented by political nonentities built around a bundle of photons, sounds and other electronic components to produce a referential effect of managed reality. This is the image we have in mind when we analyze Berlusconi's regime: fasces of electronic nothingness beaming from the TV screens.

two

The Sociopolitical Conditions
of Berlusconi's Regime

In the spring of 1994, cinematographer Vittorio Storaro supervised the restoration and U.S. re-release of *The Conformist* (1970), Bernardo Bertolucci's first mainstream hit. The title character, Marcello Clerici (Jean-Louis Trintignant), is a (homo)sexually repressed man whose desire for normalcy leads him in 1938 to join the Fascist Party and assist in the murder of his former philosophy professor. The new print included the "Dance of the Blind" (a sequence deleted for the film's initial U.S. run), which is an apt metaphor for the Italian need to unanimously follow the latest trend—any trend.

From fashion to politics, Italian society has developed an obsession with being trendy. People try to identify what is "hot" before everybody else discovers it and conforms. At the same time, people desire to be recognized as "trend-setters" and be imitated by others. The tension between trendsetters' desire for distinction and everybody else's attempt to catch up is regulated by an ideology that simultaneously creates difference and recognition. Ironically, distinction per se is not approved, unless it ultimately leads back to conformity.

The media has intensified this cultural pattern. In a social context where media connectivity defines social reality and social power is no longer determined by knowledge alone but by the ability to connect different domains of knowledge, people have come to be defined by their ability to communicate via a compatible standard, to follow and at times develop scripts and standardized discourses. The discourses themselves must then be "compatible" or "similar," conformant to guidelines set up by the dominant communication system. Sociability becomes the practice of establishing connections, of linking individuals to a fluctuating discursive infosphere. In this series of flows that is the mediascape, the individuals or groups to first recognize the emerging discursive formation take the lead in the new conformism. The hype surrounding a new trend must be immediately recognized, accepted and interiorized. The entire Italian society is involved: this is an asymptotic movement between stepping out of line to produce or recognize change and immediately returning to the line so as to not stick out too much. Enormous quantities of energy are spent to compete for "equality"; to be equal but one (conformist) step ahead of everybody else.

In Italy, the process of conformity is even more evident at the corporate level. To understand the current Italian romance with Berlusconi and Fini, it is essential to examine the role played by social corporations (families, clienteles, media groups) in the creation of the conformism necessary for implementing social connectivity. Hence, this chapter will explore a social reality where a generalized hyperconnectivity based on conformity has produced a neo-baroque environment from which Berlusconi has profited the most. In this context we will first discuss the connection between power relations (especially patronage), then we will address the political economy which made possible and still supports Berlusconi's regime, finally we will direct our attention to the hyperspectacular media technologies employed by the new regime.

For a Political Anthropology of Italian Conformism

The Italian family, often pictured as isolated and autonomous, providing a safe haven for its individual members in a world of hostile forces, is a favorite subject among social scientists, especially anthropologists. Just after World War II, an American social scientist, Edward Banfield, went to Italy to study a small town in the South. He was so amazed by what he found there that he coined the term "amoral familism" to describe the behavior of its residents. He characterized the Southern Italian peasants he studied as caring for and pursuing the interest of only their immediate, or nuclear, family. The rule they supposedly follow, the ethos of "amoral familism," was summarized as "maximize the material, short-run advantage of the nuclear family and assume that others will do likewise" (1958: 85). People were pictured as thoroughly self-serving, shortsighted and fickle, resistant to cooperation outside the family. Such a reading of Southern Italy, as Italians themselves and anthropologists were later to complain, was methodologically flawed, theoretically unsound, ethnocentric and reeked of cultural stereotypes.

Many of Banfield's ideas and ethnocentrisms have been so soundly trounced that it is difficult to say anything positive about his work. Nevertheless, we would like to draw attention to the second tenet of the "amoral ethos": "assume that all others will do likewise." This strikes at the core of commonly accepted social behavior when Italy was still a country composed of many face-to-face communities. In this context, public actions were driven by an opportunistic logic that called for taking advantage of any possible occasion to seize the biggest possible piece of the pie (job security, political influence, material resources). Failure to do so would have automatically advanced the cause of one's competitors, who were frequently those closest in rank. This social model put in place an ideology of strategic moves that called a person *furbo* [cunning, clever, shrewd] if he succeeded in manipulating the mutual rights and obligations of a particular social relationship in his own favor. On the other hand, a person was called *fesso* [foolish, stupid, gullible] if he was unable to keep others from exploiting his weakness. It goes without saying that the furbo is praised and admired, while the fesso is ridiculed (see Schneider and Schneider 1976).

From this description, it would appear that egoism and cynicism always prevailed. However, such a reading would underestimate the role played by reputation in the allocation of resources in that stratified society. Individual reputation depended on the social standing of the family, on the respect [*rispetto*] due to it, which was composed of its honor and reputation [*stima*], and was determined by community judgments of family members' attempts to conform to community norms. The community set the standards and it was only by conforming to those standards that the individual attained an identity and a sense of self-respect. Conformity, not amorality, was at the basis of this social ethos.

In a society where individuals traditionally relied on their family for both affective and material support, family values constituted the bedrock for determining social standing. The traditional family, however, must not be understood as an isolated and nuclear entity. Rather, 'the family' was immersed in a wider network based on spiritual kinship ties (godparenthood) and paternalistic ties with powerful individuals or groups. The historical shift from large, patrilineal groups to smaller, bilateral families (in other words, the shift from consanguinity to conjugality) was in fact balanced by the growth of spiritual kinship as a response to the diminishing importance of the wider ties of consanguinity. In such a situation, godparenthood and patronage regulated extra-individual action, handing down judgments on the behavior of godsons and clients.

Technologies of interactional power, such as gossip, envy [*invidia*], communal teasing and joking, anonymous accusations, or the evil eye [*malocchio*] were warnings against the ambition to distinguish oneself from one's equals; they were, as Bourdieu (1979) pointed out, a reminder of the need for class, or group, solidarity, and as such were directed at near-status equals. This concern for conformism induced an anxious quest for authorities and models of behavior, and led to choices based on "sure" and "certified" values, which in most contexts meant values handed down by patrons, i.e., people in the powerful position of regulating access to valuable resources.

The patron-client relationship is not only crucial in understanding conformist mechanisms in traditional Italian society but it is still quite valuable in understanding the contemporary situation. The emergence of the society of the spectacle has substituted traditional technologies of conformism with spectacular media technologies, such as tabloids exposés, media interviews, broadcasted parliamentary inquiries or talk shows. In these late-modern times, the ideology of conformism requires an infusion of media charisma to function properly. The traditional ideology of char-

45

ismatic patronage (more on this later), provides the rationale for accepting another man's authority and behavior as the model to which one conforms. However, today this is no longer enough: to create conformity, personal charisma must be combined with spectacular media practices and it must be connected to political patronage and financial corruption.

State Patronage and the Subterranean Government [*Sottogoverno*]

Though the patron-client relationship is coercive and exploitative, it requires solidarity and reciprocity. It is based on an inequality marked by monopolization by the patrons of economic and cultural positions of resources which are of crucial importance for the clients, such as: access to the means of production; knowledge of where power lies and how to relate to it; the ability to produce hegemonic discourses. This relationship is vertical, particularistic and diffuse; its asymmetry sets up the conditions for a simultaneous exchange of different types of resources (usually the patron provides material resources and protection in exchange for the client's support, loyalty and obedience). This is a long-term, unconditional relationship of debt, usually in opposition to the written contracts of the modern state. Patronage takes its forms from the local context where the exchange of goods and services establishes the obligation to enter social relationships with groups of different status, thus providing the conditions for a basic trust and solidarity within the community at large. The debt, expressed as interpersonal obligation, is thus directly connected to conceptions of personal identity (honor, respect, 'face') and is likely to find social expression in godparenthood rituals. The ambivalent and inherently exploitative nature of the relationship is most of the time obscured by ideological structures providing a rationale of "natural necessity." Among the pillars of this ideology is the Catholic ritual, where patronage images, such as the patron saints and the Virgin Mary, are construed as intermediaries to God, the ultimate source of patronage.

After the unification of Italy in 1860, the ties of dependency stemming from patronage were amplified by the imperfect integration of the Italian national system in community life. The existence of a malfunctioning central administration forced people to interact with a distant, impersonal and biased system that they did not comprehend. Thus, the people less competent to deal with these public institutions looked for patrons able to represent them in the bureaucratic political arena. In the context of the nation-state, patrons became powerbrokers and network manipulators, intervening in favor of their clients to have the state grant them privileges and protections.

After World War II, the ruling politicians, especially the Christian Democrats, looked to patronage as a way to entrench themselves in power and directly finance the party, freeing it from private contributions. State patronage took different forms, from the *raccomandazione*, a politician's personal reference to help somebody surmounting the obstacle of a malfunctioning bureaucratic apparatus, to the *bustarella*, the envelope filled with money that has lately escalated into an epidemic of large bribes and kickbacks, particularly in connection with government contracts. However, political patronage found its most complete realization with the construction of an economic system based on state corporations and agencies. These entities were hypothetically independent, but since they received state funds and were managed by government appointees, they were subject to political control. They included most of Italy's large industrial firms, the major banks and credit institutions, social security and welfare agencies, state radio and television corporations, hospitals, universities, research centers, opera houses, museums, as well as organizations for sport, culture and recreation. Together these public corporations reached every corner of society and touched all individuals in it. People related to this archipelago of public corporations came to be known as *sottogoverno*, meaning an underlying level of government. And people related to it in about the same way they related to the government: they sought party affiliation and political influence as a way to find a job, receive a contract, or extend their web of clients.

In the 1970s, 45,000 state corporations controlled 80 percent of banking, one fourth of industrial employment and one half of Italian fixed investment. This was the apex for sottogoverno, during which this conglomeration of public entities comprised a system of political power parallel to the elected parliamentary body. Executives were chosen less for their professional abilities than for their party allegiances and connections. Thus executives owed a debt to the political parties and such debts never went uncollected. Using this web of clientelistic relationships, the Christian Democrats extended their power throughout the country. It was not until the end of the 1970s, when the newly reformed Socialist Party of Bettino Craxi moved into this system, that the Christian Democrats' hold on the sottogoverno was loosened. For the socialists, key positions in state agencies with access to funds and patronage were more important than positions in the cabinet. With the lapsing of the 'historic compromise' in 1979, the Christian Democrats became dependent on socialist cooperation, and Craxi drove a hard bargain. By the early 1980s, the Christian Democrats had been forced to "secularize" Italian politics. They had given up half the positions in state industrial firms and controlled only 40 percent of the positions in cultural agencies and 37 percent of those in health and social welfare, but still held on to three fourths of those in banks. While the dispersion of the power of the sottogoverno was one of the most effective ways of destroying the concentration of Christian Democratic power, a simple changing of the guard did not alter a system of gross maladministration with grave economic and social effects, particularly for the business community.

Neoliberalism Protected by Political Corruption

The secularization of Italian political life in the 1980s opened the door to a new season of neoliberal corporate raids protected—and sometimes sponsored—by a increasingly greedy political class. As a result, political corruption—already well established during the decades of the Christian Democrats' regime—became the single-most important factor in the relationship between the Italian state and the business community. The incorporation of Craxi's neoliberalist strategy within the Christian Democrats' clienteles and Mafia interests simply raised the corruption level to its breaking point. By 1993, politicians were now asking for a 15 percent cut on all public contracts, and corruption had completely engulfed the highest levels of government (from the socialist ex-prime minister Craxi to the Christian Democrat ex-prime minister and senator-for-life Giulio Andreotti) as well as a number of business corporations (including, for example, the second-largest European oil and chemical company, Enimont). When a new generation of magistrates was finally able to break the silence and schemes of kickbacks and secret deals, it became apparent that virtually the entire political class who had ruled Italy since World War II would have to go to jail.

This political corruption however, was not a bizarre or pathological phenomenon: it was the result of free trade strategies taking advantage of the loosening of social rules in the postindustrial context. This kind of corruption is a structural phenomenon that occurs when immaterial production takes the lead in the economies of technologically advanced societies. In a recent research paper on the economy of corruption, French economist Michel Albert argues that when financial deals are made in a global market and shares are traded internationally via computers, the ethics underlying these late-capitalist transactions are radically different from those regulating early-capitalist transactions. "The great novelty," writes Albert, "lies in the absence of the legislator. The state has become impotent. Capital flows effortlessly from one side of the planet to the other. No one is able to track it down. The law becomes inapplicable. And bandits prosper. They are the sons of international finance" (1993: 183).

Shareholders are no longer associated with the property they have bought, or with its management. The financial cycle becomes essentially symbolic, detached from material production. A shareholder who can move his money from one country to another in the space of a few hours becomes unaccountable for the social and human consequences of his investment choices. International financial deals free investors from moral accountability, making them obey only the immaterial laws of the market.

It should not be a surprise then that the Italian business community willingly and eagerly entered a partnership with the political class for a greater profit. For instance, the pharmaceutical industries were granted hefty rises in the price of prescription drugs by the Ministry of Health, and in turn the Minister (in this case, the liberal Francesco De Lorenzo) received a share of these enormous profits directly deposited into a Swiss bank account. This was not a case of a few corrupt individuals; rather, it was a structural phenomenon. The proof of this is that even after Tangentopoli had sent an entire political class into early retirement, the politicians who took over, Berlusconi and his cronies of Forza Italia, were the direct heirs of the former corrupted system, in which they played the role of corruptors.

Berlusconi's Fininvest, Italy's second-largest private company in the 1980s, accumulated its economic power thanks to the preferred treatment it received from Craxi, who allowed generous financial loans from state banks in return for media coverage. In the spring of 1994, Berlusconi admitted that he had offered special advertising prices to socialist candidates who wanted to run ads on his networks. In exchange for this almost-free advertising, Craxi and his Socialist Party made sure that Berlusconi could have unlimited credit with the banks and could manage his media monopoly undisturbed. And the Italian people, after having condemned and vilified the corrupted Christian Democrats and Socialist politicians, voted eagerly for their principal accomplice and main media counterpart. People could not have failed to notice the structural alliance and patronage relationship between Berlusconi and Craxi, but they decided not to make an issue of it.

There are two lessons to be learned from this paradoxical attitude: the first is that some corrupted politicians can be removed, but corruption as a system connecting economic, political and financial power cannot be eradicated. The second has to do with the way Italian society handles change. The old regime has in fact been disposed of using the traditional Italian form of the passive revolution: appearing to change everything but avoiding structural changes in the very fabric of civic society.

Semiocapitalism: The Kingdom of Contingencies

As much as the decisive aspect of the Italian authoritarian turn is constituted by a nearly absolute control over the media, we should not underestimate the fact that the Right knew how to express the values, needs and expectations of a large part of the Italian workforce, namely that vast army who in the 1990s mobilized itself, creating businesses in conditions of absolute flexibility and complete dependence on the dynamics of global capitalism. These dynamics are: the acceleration of the business cycle, the unlimited expansion of the workday, the uncontrolled exploitation and abolition of social protections. In order to make the absolute willingness of the workforce possible, the neoliberal ideology highlights the identification of work with business, and gives life to a sort of mass capitalism for which the center is the stock market, and the financial capital is mobile and fungible, fragmentary and reticulated. The new workforce is no longer attracted to the prospect of a stable job, but by the dynamic flexibility and the rapid turnover that the new economy makes possible. The process of economic globalization had radically changed the expectations of workers because it has modified the very nature of work. This factor must be taken into consideration if we want to understand what has happened during the last decade, not only in Italy, but in the post-industrialized world in general.

Neoliberal ideology and xenophobic instinct are intermingled in the representation of the government's right-wing parties. This representation is an answer to the expectations of the vast part of the labor force, which sees itself as small, flexible, fragile and dynamic. The changes in the social composition of work and its ideological correlates have not been fully understood by the Left, which has been proven time and again unable to organize it.

Following the digitalization of the work process and the rise of financial capitalism, capital accumulation no longer depends on the quantifiable mass of commodities nor on the amount of labor invested in a commodity, but on the communicative and symbolic action that semiotic goods produce. Postmodern capitalism can be thought of as semiocapitalism, because now the production process directly involves the communication and production of signs. And what country could fit into a system based upon chatter, spectacle and exhibitionism better than Italy, the country of the *commedia dell'arte*? We should not forget that Berlusconi's victory was first and foremost the victory of the illusory myth of the self-made man and this myth in the 1990s had a strong hold on the sectors of innovative work, highly cognitive and relational, which was emerging from the postindustrial system. The myth of the independent businessman who succeeds in creating a personal empire, starting from nothing does not at all correspond to Berlusconi's biography, but what does that matter? Just a month before the election on May 13, 2001, virtually every Italian voter received a 100-page magazine containing the personal biography of the beloved leader of Forza Italia: Berlusconi collecting flowers, kissing children and smiling, smiling, smiling.

But what is semiocapital? The economist Christian Marazzi posits that contemporary capitalism is essentially semiotic. Language is the tool of production in the postindustrial system, the product that circulates in the veins of immaterial markets (Marazzi 2002). Another economist, Michel Albert, traces the evolution of capitalists' behavior from the industrial age to the present: in the industrial period, this behavior was characterized by a sort of *affectio societatis*, i.e., the owner's affection for his factory, for the people who worked in it, for the social utility of the concrete process of production (Albert 1993 [1991]). In the postindustrial age, on the other hand, capitalists are no longer responsible for the social good and cannot be held morally accountable. They do not care about the contents of their investment, since they only worry about the semiotic connection to their wealth and to the flow of immaterial financial transactions.

Marxist theory has always affirmed that capitalism is based on some kind of exploitation and that private property is somehow the result of theft. However, the contemporary issue is not only the systematic exploitation of workers and the stealing of surplus value, but the primacy of manipulating semiotic resources in the accumulation of semiocapital. Thomas Hobbes wrote that people are better than animals because of language, but worse than animals because they use language to lie. As the economy becomes primarily linguistic, the ability to create truthful statements factors into the production of economic value. The need to avoid the appearance of falsehood becomes the overall concern of production and exchange.

In the sphere of semiocapital, the production of capital is increasingly interlinked with processes of linguistic exchange. By means of language we can create shared worlds, express ambiguous statements, elaborate metaphors, simulate events, or simply lie. The semioeconomy is thus based on the creation of worlds, metaphorical castles, imaginary scenarios and forecasts, simulations and lies.

While the industrial economy was founded on the production of value that was objectively measurable and quantifiable on the basis of the amount of socially necessary work, the postindustrial economy is based on linguistic exchange. Simulation becomes the decisive element in the determination of value. And when simulation becomes central to the processes of production, it is possible, or rather probable, that lies, deceit and fraud will become a regular part of economic life. The Enron case is instructive in this regard. Enron's bosses, great friends and financial backers of Bush, swindled hundreds of thousands of workers, pensioners and investors by manipulating symbols, information, forecasts and valuations. They took advantage of the economic conditions created by the semioticization of capital and labor.

The semiocapitalist sphere is governed by laws that do not resemble those of the glorious era of industrial work, and by relationships that do not resemble the discipline of production, the business and work ethic that dominated the world of classical industrial capitalism, that Protestant capitalism defined by Michel Albert as "Rhenish capitalism" because its ideal geographical space was the industrial area of Germany near the French border. Recent decades have witnessed a profound transformation, beginning with the disconnection of the financial network from the real economy. The foundational moment of this process was the arbitrary decision made by Nixon to abandon the Bretton Woods system established in 1944. In 1971, the President decided to eliminate the gold standard for the U.S. dollar, thus creating the self-referentiality of the American currency. From that moment on, money fully became what it already was in essence: a sheer act of language. Money was no longer a referential sign that referred back to a lode of commodities, a quantity of golden metal, or any other given good; rather it was a factor of simulation, an agent capable of setting in action processes both arbitrary and independent from the real economy. Therefore semiocapital is the system of full indeterminacy: the financial turn of the economy and the dematerialization of production have lent to social actors an unpredictability and uncertainty before unknown in the history of the industrial economy.

As Karl Marx explained, in the industrial production process, the determination of the value of a commodity can be based on a reliable element: the amount of work socially necessary to produce that commodity. But this is no longer true in the sphere of semiocapital, where the main factors in the production of goods are cognitive labor, memory, language and imagination. Under this new model, the criterion of valorization is no longer objective, and no longer quantifiable on the basis of a fixed referent. Labor time no longer serves as an absolute touchstone. Lies, violence and corruption are no longer marginal excrescences of economic life, but tend to become the alpha and omega of the everyday business management. The criminals are in control, but no longer in the old Marxist sense (according to which property is theft, and thus the owners must have robbed something, known as the surplus value), but in a much more direct way. Economic power belongs to those who possess the most powerful linguistic machines. Government of the mediascape, dominance of software production, and control over financial information: these are the sources of economic power. Moreover, dominance of these sources of power is not established though good old competition between honest entrepreneur-exploiters, but rather through lying, deceit and war. There is no longer any economic power that is not criminal. Consequently, the Berlusconi government is not in any way the exception, but rather the new rule of the political and economic management of capital.

Berlusconi's regime is not founded on the repression of dissent or on obliga-

tory silence. On the contrary, it is founded on the proliferation of chatter, on the irrelevance of opinion and discussion, on the banalization and the ridiculization of thought, disagreement and criticism. It is true that there have been (and will continue to be with ever-greater frequency) cases of censorship, of direct repression of criticism and free thought, but these are fairly marginal incidences with respect to the essential phenomenon, which is that of an immense information overload and a true assault on attention, naturally accompanied by the occupation of all information sources by the Boss and his company.

The current social makeup of Italy cannot be compared to the predominantly peasant and rustic population of the 1920s. In the first decades of the twentieth century, the futurist modernism of the Fascist Party introduced an element of innovation and social progress, while today's regime does not contain any seeds of progress, and its economic policy is founded on the dismantling of the patrimony accumulated over the years. A perfect example is a recent law put forward by the Berlusconi government in order to meet the country's spending needs and reduce taxation. This law provides for the privatization of those state agencies that are not currently earning a profit and for a fire sale of the public patrimony. Italy holds a significant portion of the world's artistic patrimony. Thus there is much to privatize, to submit to the criteria of private profit, to sell, to devastate. While Mussolini's Fascists began a process of productive modernization of the country, the Forza Italia regime seems inclined to sell it off, just as Carlos Menem did in Argentina during the decade preceding the fall of that country's economy and society.

The Counter-Reformation and Italian Specificity

But how is Italy distinct from other Western countries in the context of contemporary Europe? Italy is the country of the Counter-Reformation, and perhaps this holds the key to understanding something about the laboratory that Italy has been in modern history. Max Weber's *The Protestant Ethic and the Spirit of Capitalism* taught us that the Protestant mentality favored the development of classic industrial capitalism. In the centuries following the Protestant Reformation, the European bourgeoisie created the foundation of their power by subjecting themselves to a rather rigid ethical and existential discipline. The bourgeois capitalist assumed responsibility for his own actions, answering for them to other men, God, and most of all, his bank manager. Economic fortune was a temporal confirmation of divine benevolence.

The Catholic Counter-Reformation on the other hand, from the Council of Trent onward, reaffirmed the primacy of the religious sphere over its secular counterpart, and reinforced the conviction that, for Catholics, observation of the ecclesiastic hierarchy was much more important than productive discipline. The deep foundation of Catholic culture resisted the bourgeoisie's fixation with productivity and efficiency. While Calvinist principles were based on respect for the law, the spirit of the Counter-Reformation reinforced the primacy of mercy and the absolute value of repentance. The Counter-Reformation remained profoundly etched on the Italian social imagination throughout the modern period, and manifested itself as a reactionary feature in crucial moments of national life: in the Neapolitan revolution of 1799, the enlightened bourgeoisie were isolated and defeated thanks to the people's complicity with Bourbon power allied to the Catholic church. During the nineteenth century, the alliance between church and the agrarian classes acted as a conservative anti-bourgeois factor and protected the cultural dominance of the Church against attempts to secularize national life. In the years following World War II, the Christian Democratic Party became the dominant political force, playing the role of mediator between capitalist modernization and populist and reactionary resistance.

In the 1970s, the formulation "Italian anomaly" was used to define the particularity of a country in which the social movements, elsewhere extinguished after 1968, held the political scene for more than a decade. During this period, the workers' resistance movement produced structures of mass organization, and fueled revolts against every effort at capitalist modernization. The Italian anomaly at that time consisted in the persistence of workers' autonomy and social conflict. Italy experienced a long season of proletarian struggles, from July 1960, when the workers in many cities rose up against the hypothetical formation of a center-right government with the participation of men connected to the old Fascist regime, to the anti-authoritarian and libertarian uprising of 1977. In all the workers' struggles for autonomy against the overlord government in factories and cities, the constant factor was the refusal of the subordination of life to work. This refusal is evident in thousands of different forms: from the stereotypical Mediterranean laziness, privileging sensuality and life in the sun over productivity and the economy, to the revolt of young workers against the rhythms of the factory, which was then transformed into endemic absenteeism and the disaffection of workers towards their jobs. The movement of *Autonomia Operaia* [Workers' Autonomy] an extraparliamentarian group that flourished from 1967 until 1977, synthesized this attitude of insubordination and resistance in the slogan "the refusal of work."

This concept of work refusal as it was used in Italy in the 1970s can be inserted within a framework of a progressive political strategy. The workers rejected the repetitive mechanical labor of the factory, and this forced companies into constant restructuring. Workers' resistance became a factor of human progress and freedom, but also an accelerator of technological and organizational development. But this should not prevent us from identifying an element of a persistent anti-Calvinism at the origin of the rejection of work. In the final analysis, the country's technical, social and cultural progress was stimulated by rejection of work, and Italian civil society reached levels of great democratic and cultural sophistication during the years when the refusal of work was most intense and the level of absenteeism in the factories at its highest. Naturally the refusal of capitalist exploitation, the opposition to increased productivity and the denunciation of workers' growing subordination were not uniquely Italian. All over the world workers wanted better wages and more free time for their own lives. All the world over, workers opposed their bosses' wish to subordinate life to work and work to profit. But it is in Italy that this insubordination became an explicit political agenda, spelled out as a political demand: resistance to work for the production of social autonomy.

At the end of the 1960s, tens of thousands of young Southern workers arrived in Turin to work for Fiat at its Mirafiori plant, the biggest and most modern car factory in Italy. They immediately became notorious for their forms of resistance to labor and anti-work attitude. In the eyes of a part of the workers movement (especially to the Italian Communist Party) as well as to the progressive industrial bourgeoisie, they appeared as a sign of ambiguous extremism. This new wave of workers had no sense of a work ethic or pride in productivity; indeed, they derided such concepts. Was this a resurgence of the *lazzarone* spirit—the individualist and anti-modernist populism of Southern poor classes, which in 1799 in Naples had caused them to oppose the revolutionary fervor of an enlightened bourgeoisie? There was an element of this, but in this lazzarone spirit there was also the conviction that the society of industrial labor was reaching its end. This idea then spread among youth culture and invaded the whole society: industrial labor was a hangover from the past; the development of technology and social knowledge opened the prospect of liberation from the society of work. The most radical components of the workers' movement expressed the conviction that industrial labor was coming to a close, and thus the alienating and repetitive form of work was no longer historically justified. This idea constituted the most radical innovation of the Italian workers' movement of the 1960s and 1970s, and the most significant departure from nineteenth-century Communist ideology.

Over the course of modernization in the nineteenth century, the Italian Left was always pulled in two opposing directions. On the one hand, a Protestant spirit, industrialist and modernist, drove it to rail against social backwardness and to demand greater productivity and efficiency from the productive system, at the price of increasing worker exploitation and promoting liberalist policies. On the other hand, an anti-productive, egalitarian and communitarian spirit led the Left to demonize capitalism and take refuge in forms of social welfare which favored parasitic policies and patron-client relationships. In the 1960s and 1970s, Autonomia Operaia wedged itself between these two tendencies of the historical Left: it incarnated a parasitic culture inscribed in the Italian cultural tradition of the lazzarone and *sanfedista* movements, but it was able to transform it creatively, thus anticipating the creative potential that would emerge at the center of postmodern and postindustrial production.

After the 1970s, workers autonomy was defeated by police repression, and the capitalist offensive of the early 1980s hit the working class in the factories with waves of layoffs, opening the way to the adoption of neoliberal ideology. But Italian-style liberalism cannot be subsumed to the bourgeois liberal tradition of Protestant derivation that flourished in modern Europe.

Liberal culture in Italy never managed to become a dominant force in Italian politics. In the nineteen century, the liberal party masterminded the *Risorgimento* [The Revival], but in reality never became the dominant culture of the Italian bourgeoisie. Italian politics in both the nineteenth and twentieth centuries were dominated by the compromise between the state and the Church, and by the alliance between the industrialized bourgeoisie and reactionary agrarian classes. Liberal culture has always championed the secularization of the state—representing a cultural element of political Protestantism and therefore always remaining in a subordinate position. In the early twentieth century, the liberal Piero Gobetti was forced to recognize that the sole possibility of liberating Italy from Catholic influence resided in an alliance between the liberal movement and the workers' movement. Unfortunately, such an alliance never came about, and fascism attacked and destroyed both the communist workers' movement led by Antonio Gramsci and the liberal movement represented by Piero Gobetti. The neoliberalism that imposed itself as the hegemonic political force from the 1980s onward has nothing to do with this liberal tradition; rather, it repurposes the alliance between all socially and culturally reactionary forces under the aegis of the ultracapitalist principle of Anglo-American laissez-faire economics.

During the 1980s, in the midst of the capitalist counteroffensive that accompanied the establishment of neoliberalism on an international level, Italy gave rise to a curious experiment in political economy. With the defeat of workers' autonomy and the social radicalism that had accompanied it, as well as the disappearance of libertarian and egalitarian social movements, the anti-Protestant ethic was transferred to the political class of the government, which bred tolerance of economic illegality, embezzlement, corruption and the Mafia. It was the time of Bettino Craxi. Although of socialist and secular background, Bettino Craxi represented the convergence of the Counter-Reformation spirit, roguish and permissive, and the cultural opening to a modernizing neoliberalism. Modernization and corruption, in the thought and practice of Bettino Craxi, were not in contradiction; rather, he saw them as two utterly complimentary tendencies, both integrated and functional.

In the 1970s, the historical Left (the Communist Party and the Catholic Left) had reacted with violence to the youth and workers' anti-Protestant refusal to work. They had accused the rebellious workers of the factories and the metropolitan youth of the social centers of hooliganism. Now, ten years later, Catholics and Communists revolted against Craxi not because he was the bearer of neoliberal and pro-business policies, but rather because of his tolerance for corruption. Bettino Craxi had felt the advancing wind of the affirmation of neoliberal doctrine. During the 1980s and 1990s, as neoliberalism gradually eliminated the old regulations of the welfare state, the defenses erected by many sectors of society to defend themselves against capitalist aggressiveness crumbled. Craxi had understood, with secular cynicism, that neoliberalism was inaugurating an era where the rules of violence, mafia, chicanery, corruption and simulation were the only rules in force. Catho-Communism, in its death throes, clung desperately to the ethical question. Instead of opposing neoliberalism, which was destroying social benefits in the country—bringing down workers' wages and imposing a competitive and for-profit culture—the center-left initiated a campaign against corruption, immorality and illegality. The Catho-Communist center-left paradoxically assumed the defense of the Protestant ethic, which was already dissolving in the culture of large-scale capitalism, as was the traditional bourgeoisie itself, to be replaced by a class of lumpenbourgeois robbers.

According to Max Weber, modern capitalism is born when citizens are conscious of the fact that their time does not belong to them but to the community. Capitalism is an affirmation of altruistic selfishness, theorized by Adam Smith as the invisible hand that regulates the market. Whoever possesses entrepreneurial capital will enjoy a privileged position and who does not will be a dependent worker. But everyone must feel themselves participants in a common endeavor: building up capital and protecting the community. The civil and religious sentiment tied to Protestantism created the cultural conditions for an acceleration of the economic development. On the other hand, those European cultural zones (such as Italy, Spain or Portugal) that remained on the margins of this revolution paid for it in the following centuries, experiencing civil and economic backwardness, political disorder and poor national cohesion.

For Max Weber, capitalism is based on some rules directly traceable to the Protestant ethic:

> Remember, that time is money.... Remember, that credit is money.... Remember, that money... can beget money.... He that kills a breeding cow, destroys all her offspring to the thousandth generation. He that murders a crown, destroys all that it might have produced, even scores of pounds. Remember this saying, "the good paymaster is lord of another man's purse" (2002: 14–15).

These are the norms upon which trust is based, an essential element of the modern bourgeois economy. But none of these norms are any longer valid for the post-bourgeois capitalist, who knows that credit does not hinge upon trustworthiness, honesty or competence, but rather on blackmail, violence and the protection offered by family and the Mafia. This is not a matter of a temporary glitch in moral rigor or of a wave of corruption. Rather it is a case of change in the deepest sense of the process of production. The determination of value has lost its objective, material base (the work-time socially necessary to produce it, as Marx said), and now depends on the games of linguistic simulation, media, advertising and semiotic production.

In a certain sense, the situation has been reversed: precisely those elements that had made Italy into a backward country now make it a laboratory of late-modern forms of power. Those forces that had placed Italy in the rearguard of modern capitalism now become the reason for its avant-garde positioning. Precisely because the culture of immoral familialism predominates, Italy becomes the cultural and political laboratory of hyperliberal capitalism. The poor penetration of state authority in the strata of society and economy had been lamented as a sign of backwardness and weakness, but the assertion of neoliberalism created a situation in which private interests, the interests of families and clans, prevail over those of the public. In the name of an ideology of pro-business and the free market, the door had in fact been left open for a sort of privatization of the state. The state machine was not reorganized as such but instead put in the service of the interests of the family. This process has not only taken place in Italy, but here the cultural conditions were especially conducive to it.

Liberal Deregulation and the Lumpenbourgeoisie

From the moment that instant profit imposed itself as the leading principle of international economic choices, political democracy has endured a collapse that mirrors the social and environmental devastations occurring all over the world.

Since the 1980s, economic deregulation has freed enormous productive energies, but at the same time it has weakened or destroyed the defenses that modern society built to protect itself from the predatory aggressiveness of capital. The modern bourgeoisie, influenced by the Protestant ethic, had mitigated the devastating thrust implicit in the logic of profit, by integrating proprietary individualism with a strong sense of community, respect for secular laws, and concern for the state which belonged to all.

The bourgeois ethic described by Max Weber is that of the capitalist-owner, who drew his profit from the expansion of his property, from the proper administration of his production, and from the utility of the products he was able to offer to the community.

On the contrary, in the postindustrial system, the interests of the capitalist are no longer identifiable with the interests of the owner. Property and profit diverge, and financial gains become the priority. As gothic and austere decorum suited proprietary capitalism, financial capitalism has a baroque look. Beginning the 1980s, the baroque spirit of the Counter-Reformation, which had hindered Southern European societies with a Catholic tradition right through the end of the twentieth century, was no longer an element of backwardness. But the Italian Left did not notice this transformation. Instead, it ended up basing all of its politics on an anachronistic moralism that exalted in a nostalgic way the bourgeois culture of modern Protestantism. In the 1970s, the Communist Party violently opposed workers' insubordination, treating it as a form of irrational extremism. In the 1980s, it made the moral question the center of its strategy, isolating itself from the lifestyles that were spreading through the groups of people involved in postindustrial production. The 1980s and 1990s saw the emergence of a new social class without bourgeois origins, which grew economically thanks to systematic illegality, tax evasion, the use of unreported workers, the payment of bribes, and in the most extreme cases, direct connections with Mafia businesses. This class had no concept of civic responsibility and as a result the public sphere was progressively undervalued and attacked, as a hindrance to the freedom of business. Whoever was less efficient in this competition without rules was marginalized, attacked and blamed. The Tangentopoli prosecutions did not at all impair this cultural group, which is indissoluble from neoliberal ideology. In the 1980s and '90s this immoral community played the role of the new entrepreneurial class.

When Berlusconi came into power, the Left could only deride the superficiality of his message; but that was precisely its strength. The Left was scandalized by the irresponsibility of the new class that emerged with Berlusconi, but this 'irresponsibility' is the spirit of neoliberal semiocapitalism; this irresponsible and arrogant style makes Berlusconi popular among the masses who think that they can gain economic advantages and social promotion. The Forza Italia class became the perfect sequel; the aggressive and violent successors of the Tangentopoli class.

In the 1980s and 1990s, the Italian image underwent a dramatic change—both in Italians' own perceptions and in the perceptions of others. Until the 1970s, they were considered good people who were generally tolerant and a little rowdy. Today, they have an image as social climbers who are cynical, presumptuous and arrogant. They were a population of emigrants whose cardboard suitcases were bound with string. Now they are considered racists who are ashamed of their own past and who try to cancel out its memory by criminalizing the poor who live across the Adriatic Sea or the Channel of Sicily. Italians have always been bereft of the strong authoritativeness of Protestants, who give the impression of having earned their good fortune with sacrifice and a fanatical work ethic. However they knew how to ride the wave of postmodernity, and some of them got rich off it, without having acquired the moderation, education or the tolerance of the rich.

How come the new hyperliberal capitalism rewards behaviors the Reformation sought to do away with; how come it rewards the immorality of the heirs of the Counter-Reformation? The ethic of this capitalism no longer has anything to do with the Protestant ethic because the forms of production and the social relations that derived from it have radically changed. The capitalist behaves less like an owner or an entrepreneur, because in fact he tends to be just the holder of shares that can be moved from one business to another. Capital valorization relies increasingly less on specific productive skills than on purely speculative competence. Corruption is no longer a casual by-product of production, but becomes an intrinsic phenomenon of an economy dominated by high finances.

Whereas the industrial entrepreneur was linked to his investment in a concrete way, so that his fortune depended on the capacity to respond to the demands of the market by improving the product, the new globalized capitalist class has no connection with the concrete productivity of its investments. To move a capital investment from Brazil to Thailand is both a simple and purely virtual gesture, not responsible for the concrete social effects it causes, the unemployment it creates, or the environmental cataclysms it can set in motion.

The modern bourgeois was linked to his business because the machines, workplace and workers were his property. Virtual capitalism separates the property from the business, and the business becomes purely financial, deterritorialized and immaterial. The global corporation can move its investment in just a few moments without having to account to its trade unions, the local community, or the government. Capital no longer has any responsibility to society nor—as we saw in the case of Enron—to its shareholders.

The Protestant ethic is no longer profitable; corruption, lies, blackmail, illegal trade and collusion with the Mafia are far more efficient. Amidst the processes of globalization, Italy is not 'disadvantaged by the illegality and immorality of its new ruling class,' as claims the moralist Italian Left. On the contrary, Italy has become the country where a neoliberal dictatorship can best flourish.

Unpredictability of Value and Neo-Baroque Society

> The reality principle corresponded to a certain stage of the law of value. Today the whole system is swamped by indeterminacy, and every reality is absorbed by the hyperreality of the code and simulation.... Capital no longer belongs to the order of political economy: it operates with political economy as its simulated model (Baudrillard 1976: 2).

The crisis of the law of value has long been corroding the foundations of capitalist society, which loses its coherence due to the development of post-mechanical technologies and the growing autonomy of workers from waged labor. In the postindustrial, networked economy the value of a commodity is determined essentially through language, and thus value is determined within the regime of simulation. The explosion of the New Economy during the 1990s was the perfect demonstration of the economic potential of simulation. Flows of imaginary capital were invested in imaginary processes of production. But this in no way meant that it was an illusion or a mirage. Networked intelligence multiplied the potential of social production, the world of commodities expanded enormously, and social desire was produced and mobilized as an economic factor.

We are entering the regime of unpredictable and fluctuating values. The mathematical regularity of the accounting books is being superseded by the unpredictability of the financial game and by the linguistic strategies and psychic implications of marketing. The economy becomes an essentially semiotic process, incorporating the indetermination that characterizes the processes of signification.

Work has become increasingly fractalized. After the end of the great industrial concentrations, the new workers, delocalized in the suburbs of the planet, have tended more and more to become computerized and cellularized terminals of the circulation of sign-like commodities. Devoid of the clear contours of industrial society, fragmented in atomized workplaces, these 'net slaves' have undergone two parallel processes. On one hand, their existence has been physically and culturally individuated from other existences. Each worker follows her trajectory and competes individually on the market. At the same time, each worker perennially finds herself in conditions of cellular connection. Every individual is a cell that the network places in constant connection with others, guaranteeing a deterritorialized, fractal and fluid sociability. The cellular network is the new production line, devoid of any elemental embodied sociability.

Simulation and fractalization are essentially baroque concepts. In the postmodern epoch, the rationalist equilibrium of industrial architectures has been replaced by the proliferation of points of view. In a book titled *L'età neobarocca* [The Neobaroque Age] published in 1991, Omar Calabrese formulates the hypothesis that the postmodern style recuperates some aesthetic and discursive models developed by baroque culture during the sixteenth century. The baroque can be best understood by analyzing its insistence on always having multiple points of view. While Protestant rigor produced an essentialized aesthetic and an austere image, the baroque declared that the divine generation of forms is irreducible to political, mathematical, architectonic, or social rules. As Deleuze says, the baroque is the plait, the fold—namely it is the poetics that best corresponds to the unpredictability of fluctuating values. When the great modern narratives lost coherence and the law of value dissolved into an unending proliferation of products, simulacra and speech acts, postmodern mythologies began to overlap in the social imaginary. Production and signification increasingly becomes a single process. But as a result of this interlacing of economics and semiotics, we are currently witnessing a crisis of economic referentiality (the relationship between value and socially necessary worktime) and a crisis of semiotic referentiality (the denotative relationship between signifier and signified). Value can no longer refer to worktime, because the time of immaterial labor is not reducible to a socially average norm, unlike what was going on in Marx's times. At the same time, the denotative relationship between signifier and signified is suspended for good in social communication. Advertising, politics and the media speak a declaredly simulated language. Nobody believes in the truth of public statements any more. The value of the commodity is fixed on the basis of simulation in a relationship that no longer has any rules.

The Diffused Force of Hyperspectacle

In the spectacular society, the imaginary energies are channeled away from real life to fill the dreamlike world of spectacle—a dimension viewed as non-lived life. On this subject, Guy Debord writes:

> The spectacle manifests itself as an enormous positivity, out of reach and beyond dispute. All it says is: "Everything that appears is good; whatever is good will appear." The attitude that it demands in principle is the same passive acceptance that it has already secured by means of its seeming incontrovertibility, and indeed by its monopolization of the realm of appearances (1994 [1967]: 15).

Through this incontrovertibility and monopolization, the spectacle has become an active force for production, and for promoting hyperspectacular simulations. The mandatory optimism of Berlusconi is linked with the construction of a perfectly orderly television studio:

> Berlusconi's totalitarian nature, which can be seen in his obsession for minute detail, keeps him in check. He has an enormous need for rationality, and responds to emotional disorder with a compulsion for order. His personal bodyguards must see that his watch dogs do not spoil the garden with their poop, since he would not tolerate a messy lawn. Fallen leaves must be collected every morning. The pillows on his mansion's many couches have one, and only one, place. In his salons, butlers hurry to straighten them as soon as a guest gets up. Each of the house's fifty-two telephones must have a felt pen next to them,

placed in the center of a white notebook. If he finds something out of order, there will be trouble! Order and cleanliness must be pursued with total rigor (Corrias, Gramellini, and Maltese 1994: 25) [our translation].

Berlusconi viewed the world as a television studio where everything had to be in order. But this need for order was a hyperspectacular, and not a militaristic, obsession: this was the order of perfect fiction, so perfect as to render reality obsolete.

In this hyperspectacular landscape, political necessities and difficult decisions were replaced by a simulated world where appearances were paramount and power filtered through smooth reflecting surfaces. In this context, the less a political formation was weighed down by ideological baggage, the more it could reflect any image, wear any mask, fulfill any expectation, become the target of any illusion and projection. In this context, informed consent was no longer necessary, just as the reasoned agreement of a majority over a specific issue or a specific project was no longer needed. Consensus had been replaced by the polled void, and this void constituted the essential condition for reinforcing the power technologies of hyperspectacle. For Berlusconi to rule, he did not need to govern. To obtain the support of a majority of voters increasingly enraptured by fantasy worlds, increasingly attracted to games of simulation, it was no longer necessary to have their educated consent. It was enough to influence their social imagination.

Polls were perhaps the best examples of Berlusconi's conversion of social reality into a virtual environment projected on the screen of everyday life. The extensive use of polls had been one of his most successful, and hyperspectacular, contributions to Italian politics. Polls, especially political ones, do not discover anything; rather, with a snowball effect, they set in motion a production of fictitious opinions.

During the electoral campaigns of 1994, 1996 and 2001, the constant broadcast (on networks owned by Berlusconi) of political polls (commissioned by Berlusconi from Berlusconi's polling agency) were determinant in shifting significant percentages of voters towards Forza Italia. In a country obsessed with riding the latest cultural wave, where being with the trend is much more appealing than declaring one's dissent from the perceived dominant opinion, successive polls pointing to people's increasing support of Berlusconi, became a clear indication to vote for him. Berlusconi used the inherent conformism of the Italian people to shape their opinion.

Berlusconi's main pollster in 1994 was Gianni Pilo, another thirty-nine-year-old self-made man, who had worked as a waiter and an appliance salesman before landing a job with Fininvest's research and marketing office. His experience with polling had begun in going door to door, ringing bells, shaking hands and shoving household appliances down northern Italian housewives' throats. One hundred days before the election, Pilo was asked to move to Forza Italia's headquarters to start Diakron, a polling institute with a dozen assistants, a handful of computers and fifty telephone lines. At the end of every hard-working day, he would deliver his results to the complacent private newscasts: "Berlusconi has 24 percent support." The next day: "He is at 25.4 percent." Then "26.5 percent," then "27.6 percent" and on and on in a magnificent daily increase. Accused by Berlusconi's opponents of forging the data, he replied: "I feel sorry for them, but we work scientifically." In the summer of 1994, the International Society of Statistics expelled Pilo for unethical behavior, but by then he was already a millionaire.

Polls work by projecting a virtual reality onto still-unformed opinions. They substitute the real world for a simulated one, and then, little by little, they seal this simulated world from outside intervention, making it impervious to real concrete situations. The political sphere and public opinion become infected by the projections stemming from the media's broadcasting of simulated events into the collective mind and the public sphere becomes a shared simulacrum.

Power Through Joy

Videocratic power is not exerted through the transmission of ideological content, or through persuasive rhetoric. It does not aim to build informed consent, rather it strives to create waves of impressionistic feelings. Informed consent means shared meaning, and in the society of the hyperspectacle, social communication has little to do with meaning and much to do with the creation of pervasive environments to which individuals are unwittingly subjected.

Traditional political propaganda acted as a persuasive machine, presenting a program, goals and values that could be shared by a majority of the population. Today, this model no longer functions. Contemporary tactics of political messages, borrowed from advertising techniques, have evolved to target cognitive forms. Advertising has in fact abandoned any pretense of informing consumers about the quality of a product in favor of a more manipulative strategy able to shape people's needs and desires. New techniques create aesthetic worlds rather than referential ones through quick-cut clips and sound bites. Until recently, the shortest edit duration considered comprehensible was two seconds. Anything shorter was thought to be too quick for an audience to make sense of. Today, video sequences (not only in commercials but also in myriad television programs, from music videos to sports and infotainment shows) regularly use edits as short as one third of a second and "flash frames" that might last as little as one tenth of a second. The increase in the amount of frames per second that present-day viewers can process allows the medium to fully exploit its element of discontinuity: viewers have learned to draw instant connections between successions of images taken from multiple contexts in different realities. However, the result of this absorption is not information but pure sensation.

Political advertising has followed suit: the images from a politician's career can be strung together and viewed in rapid succession to morph into a new image directly in tune with the cognitive and sensible expectations of today's media viewers.

We live in the Age of Disenchantment. Yet, disenchantment is not cynicism, nor is it the abandonment of any hope or faith. Disenchantment is the suspension of faith. Faith has lost its object, but the expectation of a better life remains. This is where Berlusconi comes in. Forza Italia's victories have been the victories of a communication strategist broadcasting a sort of mandatory optimism. Berlusconi's appeal has continually banked on the public's disenchantment, upon which he has built an image of irrepressible optimism. While the center-left intellectualized a Beckett-like desertification of moral life, Berlusconi promoted optimistic self-delusion (e.g., "one million new jobs!") and anachronistic family values that nobody practiced anymore but in which everybody wanted to believe.

Berlusconi charmed with his television channels and his agents emanating psychic fluxes to soothe anxiety, trivialize the unknown, and transform nonlives into virtual lives in the name of a mandatory optimism. All totalitarian phenomena have made use of mandatory optimism. Nazism's cultural politics were based on the insistent exaltation of German happiness and joyful German community. Goebbels' strength consisted in mixing the persecution of the losers with the vitalized hysterics of the winners. "*Kraft durch Freude*" [power is reached through joy] concluded Goebbels, declaring that National Socialism must be a cultural movement for organizing optimism.

True to Goebbels' spirit, during a televised interview Berlusconi declared, "to transmit intensity you must first feel it. Force is contagious, as is optimism. I came up with an expression that I like to repeat to my collaborators: you must feel like the sun is in your pocket." In this spirit, Berlusconi's networks have created a fantasy world that people relate to with naïve merriment.

Berlusconi talks the same language used by scores of clerks lost in nine-to-five drudgery, by small businesses oppressed by taxes, by young people scared for their future. He knows how to keep things simple, especially with numbers: if elected, he said in 2001, he would create one million new jobs in the first six months, lower direct taxes to 30 percent, reduce the deficit by two points a year, reduce the current 200 taxes to ten simple ones. Perfect numbers illustrating simple programs: a trick learned from voodoo Reaganomics.

Berlusconi appeals to average citizens—they admire his ability as a self-made man, his cleverness in juggling legality and illegality, his disregard for laws and regulations and his dexterity in getting away with it all. He admitted belonging to the illegal Masonic lodge P2, but he was not prosecuted. He gained and used Craxi's protection, but survived the latter's demise. Berlusconi is considered a cunning and lucky person, two qualities viewed as indispensable to survive in Italy.

As with Mussolini, but unlike Hitler, people look at Berlusconi as 'one of us,' someone not radically different from the average person, maybe just a little better. Berlusconi shares the middle class's entrepreneurial vitality, ferocious pragmatism and cheerful cynicism. Only his boundless narcissism puts him on a higher platform. "Every morning," he once said during a convention speech, "I look in the mirror and I repeat aloud: 'I like myself, I like myself, I like myself.' Remember: if you like yourself you will be liked by others." During the 2001 electoral campaign, responding to a society journalist in search of colorful details, he answered: "My worst defect? Let's see... to tell the truth, I can't think of any." His upbeat tone and optimistic outlook originate from his narcissism. People are not scared by his attitude, they recognize it as a feature of a winner.

Berlusconi plays the role of the sibling. Let's not forget that in Italy the relationship with the brother (for both men and women) is the least problematic relationship an individual can have within the family. However, as with all brothers, Berlusconi can be despotic. People working for him have to learn to live with his dictates and fixations, such as his abhorrence of facial hair. When Berlusconi bought the AC Milan football team, he asked all players to shave daily and discouraged beards, moustaches and long hair (the only exception he made was for World Champion Ruud Gullit's dreadlocks). The same happened with his television companies: no bearded men could be seen on video. He also imposed a "Fininvest uniform" for all his employees, later extended also to Forza Italia's candidates: blue suit, short hair and a tie. In the 1993 general elections he went as far as to provide a kit for all candidates: a small suitcase (the sort given out at conventions) containing Forza Italia's booklets (with answers for all possible election questions), a banner and pins with the colors of the Italian flag and three ties.

Berlusconi was among the first politicians to realize that in a world increasingly concerned with surfaces, image is the ultimate object for determining individual worth. Reporters have made fun of Berlusconi's maniacal attention to detail, but his insistence on the right look—something he learned from his media business— has given him a clear advantage against his political opponents, especially during televised debates.

Language, Politics and Advertising

How has political language lost its efficacy? Why has the majority of the Italian population been able to identify with a power that makes arbitrary use of words by establishing their meaning in a random and ambiguous manner, always redefinable, according to interests and circumstances, with no respect for referentiality and objective truth? What has happened to political language, and why does Berlusconi seem to possess the key to speaking the language of the postpolitical, of which the Left is ignorant? Let us try not to forget that this man comes from the realm of advertising and that he has made his fortune in the management of a company named *Publitalia* [trans. note: the Italian word for advertising is *pubblicità*, thus the name of Berlusconi's company is a fusion of that word with *Italia*]. In this realm, language has a unique mode of operation: the principle of the verifiability of pronouncements is suspended, and linguistic signs have an ambiguous, polysemic value. This is because the advertising pronouncement does not have the character of accurate information, and signs go beyond a denotative function: advertising language institutes its own world of reference, it evokes it, simulates it, suggests it. Berlusconi has deeply assimilated the logic of advertising, and he has transferred the style and the techniques of that language into political communication.

With advertising, we enter a regime characterized by the indeterminacy or randomness of the relationship between signifier and signified, in which it is not possible to fix the semantic value of a sign, object or word without referring to context and intent: "Today the whole system is swamped by indeterminacy," Baudrillard tells us, "and every reality is absorbed by the hyperreality of the code and simulation. The principle of simulation governs us now, rather than the outdated reality principle. We feed on those forms whose finalities have disappeared. No more ideology, only simulacra" (1993: 2). For this reason, critical thought is powerless against the dominant imaginary of the video-electronic age. The dominant imaginary can only be deconstructed via a mythopoetic means, not through the critical reestablishment of an original truth. There is no original truth in the world projected by advertising and television communication.

In the past, the image was a rare and precious representation of a truth to remember or celebrate (one thinks of sacred icons); the signifier and the signified aspired to closeness, to a reciprocal incarnation without residuals. When the image is produced at the fast pace of photo, film and television reproduction, or when the image enters the digital dimension, we see how representation decidedly cedes to simulation. At that point, critical judgment finds itself out of place, inadequate, impotent.

Everyone knows very well that advertising is not designed to inform us or to tell us the truth. No one is stupid enough to believe that we will be happy because we use toilet paper X, or that we will have a serene old age if we are clients of bank Y. However, this does not mean that the advertising message is ineffective. Its effectiveness is manifested not at the level of veridicality, but by its suggestive capacity. The advertisement suggests aesthetic, psychological and contextual values from which we do not know how to escape.

The excessive language of the crazy Berlusconian escapades functions according to advertising logic, and this produces a kind of gigantic political trompe l'oeil. We believe that we are more-or-less dealing with a classical parliamentary democracy and normal elections, in a condition of free opinion-making. But this belief does not correspond with reality. When an advertising and television apparatus locates itself at the center of the political scene, when the flow of public discourse originates from a source accustomed to using the language of advertising while political adversaries remain bogged down in the argumentative logic of political assemblies, at that point you cannot win by opposing reason to the absurd, using facts to construct deformations. Rather, the critical exercise appears almost ridiculous, as if someone intended to contest the "truth" of an advertisement. Do we want perhaps to contest the truth of the pronouncement: "Salia, the mint that kills"? Do we want to argue the request of the blonde woman who tells us: "Call me Peroni, I'll be your beer"? Do we want to put into doubt the fact that good God in heaven drinks Lavazza coffee?

Ubu Rex

During the summer of 2003, Berlusconi's government reached what could be considered the apex of its leader's public persona—a blend of comedy, exaggeration, vulgarity, stupidity and aggressiveness. The opposition was scandalized like boarding school girls before a pervert exposing himself in public. In early July, the European Parliament convened to solemnly celebrate the beginning of the Italian presidency of the Union. Italy's prime minister, Cavalier Berlusconi, was about to assume the role of president of the European Council. In the preceding days, press from all nations had remarked upon the Italian anomaly, the absurdity of a nation governed by the same person who controls the entire communications system. The press expressed considerable fear regarding the strange notion that the man who would represent the European Union seemed to represent only his own interests, or at the most, the strategic interests of the United States—a rival, if not exactly enemy, power. Thus Berlusconi's opening address was awaited with a certain curiosity and trepidation. And the trepidation was warranted, because after a certain number of predictable banalities, the Cavalier uttered some of his more astonishing gaffes, managing to offend and scandalize the entire European political world.

While awaiting the beginning of Berlusconi's speech, several European deputies of the Socialist and Green Left, intending to denounce the recent measures taken by the center-right Italian government to guarantee the immunity of its prime minister, had raised signs that read: "The law is the same for all." Berlusconi mocked and sneered at this protest. In particular, he got into it with a German social-democratic deputy, and he told him that he could be an extra in a film on concentration camps, because he looked and was behaving like a *Kapo*. The entire Parliament was astounded. How could Berlusconi say something like that? It was not thinkable within the catalog of pronounceable phrases of a representative of Europe. Was the jolly Italian president joking about Nazi concentration camps? Was he perhaps thinking he could use the Holocaust as a polemical argument, or as derision? To downplay the remark, Berlusconi declared that in Italy, a land of spirited people, it is entirely normal to tell jokes about the Holocaust. Someone remarked that perhaps telling jokes about the extermination of the Jews is the habit among people with whom Berlusconi associates, not of Italians in general. Several days later, the Undersecretary of Tourism of the center-right Italian government found a way to insult German tourists, who he said were rowdy and burped after drinking hectoliters of beer in Italian restaurants. Prime Minister Schroeder promptly canceled his vacation in Italy. The paradoxical, but perhaps intentional effect, of Berlusconi's latest scandal was to divert attention from the main accusation of the German parliament: namely that Berlusconi was exploiting his parliamentary majority in Italy to put himself above the law.

Also during these weeks, political leaders of the Northern League with institutional responsibilities had proposed shelling the ships transporting illegal immigrants toward Italian shores. And so on and so forth with such nonsense. All summer long, the representatives of the Italian government seemed engaged in a struggle of verbal violence and vulgarity that to some seemed a sign of political self-mutilation, to others a sign of simple ignorance. Political commentators predicted a rapid government crisis and a plummet in the faith of the voters. Such a scenario might indeed occur, sooner or later, and the confusion and frenzy would render the situation intolerable. But weren't they missing something here? Wasn't there perhaps something that went beyond the language of politics and institutions?

Are we sure that the violation of linguistic taboos of officialdom had a negative effect on the political consensus that the center-right majority enjoyed, and in particular on its theatrical director, Silvio Berlusconi? It has not been at all proven: indeed, many things seem to indicate that the Italian people like such provocations, whether they are intentional or not. Undoubtedly, the word choice and the style of the men who composed his government was the object of international embarrassment and open scandal in the press, progressive as well as moderate. But what did the people think? Are we sure that Berlusconi and his government would lose support because they acted in such an informal, clumsy and uncultivated manner? What if the opposite were true? Perhaps the majority of the Italian electorate enjoys a prime minister who gives the horns to a Spanish diplomat while they pose for an official photo, or who declares that Rome was "founded by Romulus and Remulus" [trans. note: the correct name of the second mythical founder of Rome is Remus]. Perhaps the majority of the Italian electorate felt tenderness toward a prime minister who said to his Danish colleague: "You are a very handsome man, even more handsome than the man whispered to be my wife's lover."

To the plebian coarseness of Berlusconi and his jolly government tablemates, the Left has for a while responded with moral indignation, with expressions of shock at the violations of politically correct language. But this outrage had not turned out to be an effective argument against the politics of the center-right government. Indeed, one might suppose that part of Berlusconi's success in politics was due precisely to this excess. This government's excessive statements and actions led to its triumph in the mass imagination of the voters. Though what exceeded the bounds of the predictable, the tolerable and the sphere of codified political behavior may have created some dismay and indignation, at the same time, it constituted a kind of pass for the legislation of the government for the effective dilapidation of the collective good, for the abolition of the rights of workers, for the imposition of discriminatory and racist laws. The technique of excess had been well-tested: one needed to talk big, very big, in order to then achieve what was essential for the accumulation of power and for the privatization of every social space. A minister who assumed the task of acting the ham, the crazy, and proposed to bombard the boats that carry immigrants toward Italian shores? Yes, he provoked scandal, but also a happy distraction: look how, soon afterward, another minister, more moderate and realist, proposed and obtained the military control of the coasts; look how a zealous functionary expelled Kurds and Syrians who sought political asylum, without even examining their requests and without respecting their rights; look how employers trampled daily on the most basic rights of foreign workers.

Humpty Dumpty in the Government

The behavior of Berlusconi's second government was incomprehensible to the conservatives of the Right and Left who thought politically according to the traditional models. These people considered a respect for dignified language indispensable, and could not imagine a context of political action other than the respect of legality. But the strength of Berlusconian media-populism consisted precisely in the systematic violation of the taboos connected to political officialdom and legality.

Influential people, such as presidents Oscar Luigi Scalfaro and Carlo Azeglio Ciampi in their frowning seriousness, were the best examples of this incomprehension of the new character of the post-political language inaugurated by Berlusconi.

What appeared most intolerable and provocative to the custodians of severity was the ridicule of the political rhetoric and its pompous rituals, which Berlusconi manipulated in a crafty and systematic manner. But there was reason to believe that the vast majority of the people who constituted the "public" of politics (the voters) were amused by his provocative and arrogant gestures, and in many cases they were won over by them: they identified with the crazy Berlusconi, the rogue prime minister who resembled them a bit, as in other ages not so far away they identified with Mussolini and Craxi. The majority of Italian voters grew up as television watchers in the age when the television became the primary vehicle of informality, of vulgar and licentious allusion, of ambiguous and aggressive language. For this reason, they were spontaneously attuned not only to Berlusconi's language, to his words and gestures, but also to his disdain for rules in the name of a spontaneous energy that the rules should not curb. The language of Berlusconi seemed made to ridicule, not to deny, not to reestablish a truth or to affirm new principles. His intention was to reveal the hypocrisy of political rules. For Berlusconi, the meaning of words was not very important, such that it was his habit to deny his own statements published in the papers the following day. Often Berlusconi pretended to approve the words of the President of the Republic, even if there was evidence that these words plainly contradicted his conduct or the legislative activity of his government. The political word was devalued, ridiculed, captured in a kind of three-card monte, in a semantic labyrinth in which every word could mean the opposite of the sense given to it in the dictionary. But it was not an effective reaction to be shocked by informality, vulgarity and superficial lies. These were elements of strength for Berlusconi and his regime, because on this level the voters understood him much better than did his political opponents (or *The Economist*).

According to common thought, political language has always obscured reality, it has always offered a hypocritical cover to the will and the bullying of the rich and powerful. Berlusconi unveils this hypocrisy in a paradoxical manner. He is the rich, powerful man who with his actions demonstrates that the law can do nothing; he is the rich, powerful man who mocks the hypocrisy of the person who pretends that the law is equal for all. Everybody knows full well that the law is not equal for all: we know from experience that those who have money and power can hire expensive lawyers, impose their interests and conquer spaces of power that are not accessible to the majority of the population. This however is habitually hidden behind the smokescreens of legality and judicial formalism. Berlusconi says with absolute clarity: I do what I want, and I laugh at the legalists who want to oppose their formalities to my will. Now that the scoundrel has in his hands the power to make and unmake laws, he uses this power to show everyone the impotence of the law. Just like Humpty Dumpty, Berlusconi knows that the meaning of words does not matter, but rather who is the boss of them. The boss of words decides their meaning, not the semantic court. The boss of the laws decides their interpretations, not the judicial court. The political spectators (the voters) seem to recognize themselves in this game of unveiling the hypocrisy of political language, even if he who reveals that "the king is naked" has paradoxically put on the pants of the king. People laugh about what

King Log says, but laugh with complicity, because King Log is declaring precisely the falsehood and hypocrisy of the words that he himself is emitting, with that tiny smile and a wink that seem to say continually: "Here I say it and here I deny it."

Before the 2001 elections, Silvio Berlusconi presented himself in one of the most widely watched televised transmissions and proposed that Italians enter into a contract with him. "Elect me and I will work to do a series of things that are written on this piece of paper," he said. Disdainful of the ridiculousness of this gesture, he pulled out a fountain pen and under the eye of the television camera, he signed his contract with Italians. None of the promises on that paper were kept: the economic situation got worse, public works were postponed until better times, legislative activity became prevalently dedicated to reinforcing his own power and protecting him against the magistrate. But nobody cared. In July 2003, as a guest at George Bush's ranch, Cavalier Berlusconi recounted this episode to Laura Bush: "Just like that, I signed a piece of paper on television. It was a huge success."

The very boring opponents of Berlusconi wanted to reestablish the sacredness of power at the same time that Berlusconi was disgracing it. Always lacking in authoritativeness, Berlusconi's government exerted its authority: it legislated in every field, including immigration, workers' rights and the justice system, everywhere imposing the logic of its predominant interests, reducing social spending, transferring wealth from the working classes to the owning classes. And none of the devastating laws promulgated by his government were stopped by parliamentary opposition or by the protests of a moderate and democratic public.

Italy: A Borderland Between Media Technopower and Ethnobarbarism

Since the second Berlusconi government was installed on May 13, 2001, the opposition forces have sought to understand and define the nature of this regime. While it seemed to bear a strong resemblance with Mussolini's fascist regime, it had many elements of continuity with the corrupt but liberal system that was created by the socialist Craxi in 1980s and 1990s.

Since the Milanese Cavalier crowned himself emperor, thanks to his domination of the media landscape and the social imagination, Italy's new regime is the synthesis of two forms of authoritarian power: the archaic and the hypermodern. On the one hand, the regime has profited and further developed an advanced system of techno-media control; on the other hand, it has allowed the reemergence of archaic identity representations that are artificially produced yet effective. In the new regime, these two strands are simultaneous and assist one another reciprocally. The hypermodern form of power based on videocracy (as represented by prime minister Silvio Berlusconi and his party, Forza Italia) is flanked by the archaic form expressed either as the aggressive affirmation of a fictional national identity proposed by the direct descendants of Mussolini's fascism, Alleanza Nazionale, or as the ethnic intolerance and economic neoliberal selfishness brought by the Lega Nord, the secessionist movement of Northern Italy. Both Alleanza Nazionale and Forza Italia contained more libertarian components, which counterbalanced the authoritarianism of some sectors of the coalition. As a party heavily involved in illegal business deals, Forza Italia had no love for law and order, at least as it applied to their leaders, who appeared disinclined to be held accountable by the courts for their activities. Moreover, the Lega Nord aspired to the dissolution of national unity, and for many years advocated the secession of the rich North from the rest of Italy. This declaredly anti-nationalist element coexists alongside the former Fascist Party, which made national unity their most fundamental value. This coexistence is both mysterious and contradictory, and yet perseveres, because beyond the programs and declarations of principle, the real objective of all participants in this government has been the dolling out of power and the looting of the *res publica*.

The cultural and political opposition forces have not reached a univocal definition of the regime, nor of strategies that might arrange its defeat. Two positions are identifiable among the opposition. There are those who have always radically repudiated neoliberal policies and corporate capitalism, and then there are others who oppose this government precisely in the name of the values and the objectives of neoliberalism. The former think that deep down, the Berlusconi government does not represent a significant novelty: the social policies it pursued follow the same thrust as those of preceding governments, whether they were center or center-left. For some time there has been substantial convergence between all political forces on a fundamental point: the capitalist principle of competitiveness has become the sole deciding factor, and the pursuit of maximum profit has absolute primacy over the needs of society. Seeing as this principle had already been adopted by the government of the center-left that governed the country between 1996 and 2001, Berlusconi's government can be seen as doing nothing more than magnifying a tendency that existed prior to his victory.

Many others believe that this government represents a radical novelty, a breach of constitutional legality and an intolerable offense against the fundamental values of democracy, good taste and good manners. In the first months of 2002 a substantial part of the democratic public organized as the so-called 'human chain movement' (known locally as *caroselli*), a large opinion group outraged and rebellious against the regime's corruption and the disdain it showed toward the fundamental rules of democratic life. This sector of the public saw the center-right government as a radical break with historical precedents and did not hesitate to use the concepts of "fascism" or "Mafia" to characterize this regime. Who is right? The former—the coherent, time-old critics of capitalism who see Berlusconi and his acolytes as the latest point in a long line of liberal robbers—or the latter—those who oppose an antisocial regime only because they see fascism reborn or the support of the Mafia?

Berlusconi's second government undoubtedly contains cultural elements of fascism and the Mafia: he is suspected of having founded his economic power on Mafia money; the entourage of the Council President consists of men who have drawn their power from the systematic exercise of illegal activities. But with respect to his first government in 1994, there is something new, namely the international context in which this government inserts itself. Today, we are at the culmination of a long period of neoliberal hegemony on a global level. This hegemony has generally devastated the social defenses that were formed thanks to the workers' struggles of the twentieth century. But this prolonged hegemony has also provoked a profound economic crisis. War has become the cultural and political horizon of the first decade of the new millennium. We cannot understand what is occurring in Italy without considering the absolute subordination of this government to the Bush II presidency, and without keeping in mind that neoliberal devastation has corrupted the foundations of social and economic life to such a degree that only terrorism and war can allow the liberalist class to maintain its power.

The Bush II presidency is not merely a continuation of the neoliberalism that governed the United States from the days of Reagan through those of Clinton. Nor, however, is it something radically new. It was born in order to continue in the same direction as the neoliberal policies of the last twenty-five years—with its constant shift of income from the working classes to the upper classes, monopolistic concentration despite the rhetoric of the free market, systematic deregulation and destruction of the social defenses against the aggressive nature of big capital—but faced with a disastrous economic crisis and no apparent way out, the dominant group of global capitalists inaugurated a policy of permanent war.

Only within this context can we understand the nature of Berlusconi's second government. Berlusconi's regime incorporates behavior from fascism (police brutality, irresponsibility, servility) and from the Mafia (contempt for the public good, tolerance of illegal economic practices). But it is not fundamentally definable as a re-creation of the fascist regime or a Mafia system. Its basic ingredients are media populism and an aggressive neoliberalism, and it functions as an objective laboratory for the cultural and political forms that accompany the formation of semiocapital.

For its long tradition of Counter-Reformation cynicism and its ethical flexibility that makes its ruling class perfectly compatible with the unpredictable system of semiocapital, Italy has become the laboratory for the new forms of global power. It is the best example of the aggressive economic policies of neoliberalism, which destroys society's defenses, disperses the collective patrimony in order to turn it into private profits. But it is also marked by the widespread tolerance of illegal activity, and the generous giveaway of promises and shared kickbacks.

The center-left opposition sees the weak point of the Forza Italia regime in its propensity for disruptive scandal and an unacceptable violation of the rules and laws. Yet actually this dazzling aggressiveness is precisely where its strength lies. The regime does not lose its consensus because it clearly shows its immoral nature. A good part of Italian society voted for it for precisely that reason. Voters chose it out of intolerance of the slowness of state agencies, bureaucracy and legalese that have slowed the dynamic thrust of the postindustrial productive system. Because of this inability to go beyond a puritanical disdain for Berlusconi's regime and unable to attack Berlusconi's venality, a technocratic centre-left, purged of its Marxist past, seems unable to mobilize support or to inspire anyone— its only viable strategies being compromises and claims to the high moral ground.

The only real opposition to the regime is deployed by the cohorts of Italian media activists, whom we now turn to in our exploration of communication and power in contemporary Italy.

three

Italian Media Activism in the 1970s

As in much of the world, in recent decades Italy witnessed the emergence of a self-organized movement of media activism among knowledge and communication workers. This media activism expressed itself through an ensemble of communicative practices aiming to remove social communication from the passivity of the spectacle in order to produce creative, public and socially engaged works. As the means of production and distribution for media discourse became more complex, costly and concentrated in the hands of few corporations, technologically mediated social communication was in the process of becoming a privatized and exclusive field. In recent years this trend has ebbed. Thanks to reduced media production costs, the capillary diffusion of technological knowledge and the increased availability of data-transfer networks, the mediascape is no longer the exclusive property of large private and public corporations, but is also populated with the experiments and exchanges of grassroots groups, individuals, artists, political and cultural agitators. Media activism came to represent the conscious practice of those who invaded the field of technologically mediated social communication to produce critical thinking and social awareness. In doing so, it fought a hard battle to redirect the social imaginary of media audiences away from the ephemeral fantasies of the media conglomerates.

Communication Technologies and Social Change

The means of techno-communicative production have played an essential societal role since the beginning of modernity. We recall how important the spread and popularization of books and the printed word were for the birth of modern society: print allowed a new dominant form of discourse, based on the bourgeois democratic values of decision-making and political action, to become easily accessible to increasingly large sectors of the population. Only when it became possible to distribute one's own thoughts and memories in written form to a substantial part of society could the nation-state take hold over large swaths of the geographical and imaginary landscape.

Between the nineteenth and twentieth centuries, new visual and audio reproduction technologies increased our ability to produce media messages and communicate with one another, resulting in a thickened infosphere with greater access to the social imaginary. For a long time, these means (photography, cinema, radio and television) remained inaccessible to the vast majority of the population because they were expensive and scarce. As a result, a narrow group of specialists was able to secure control over the totality of semiotic production. However, beginning in the 1970s, these instruments of techno-communicative production began to be mass produced and marketed affordably, thus becoming accessible to an ever-greater number of people. Such mass production and circulation produced a democratization of semiotic production, which counteracted the concentration of the means of communication in the hands of a few media conglomerates.

One of the first technologies to appear in the hands of the social movements was the mimeograph. The mimeograph was used primarily for the rapid mobilization of a considerable number of people through the reproduction of thousands of copies of messages at lightning speed and bargain prices. Leaflets with calls for a political action—including background information and slogans for a strike or demonstration—were written in the evening and then five thousand copies were pressed during the night, ready to be distributed in the morning at the gates of a factory, on the steps of a university hall, or in the center of town. The massive circulation of political messages in 1968 depended on the use of the mimeograph, which during those years made informal, wild, and independent consciousness-raising capillary actions possible—a phenomenon that would not have been possible with the traditional tools of the rotary press.

Three crucial tools for the widespread access of semiotic production followed shortly after the mimeograph: the offset press, the radio and the video recorder.

The offset machine facilitated the printing of a limited number of copies of color newspapers, with a livelier layout, richer colors, and more imaginative format than the mimeograph. The proliferation of 'transversal' newspapers and journals (such as A/Traverso, ZUT and hundreds of other news sheets and fanzines) that characterized the explosion of the autonomous creative movement between 1975 and 1977 was made possible by the low cost and easy-to-use nature of the offset press, which permitted layout assembly in the absence of printing expertise and allowed alteration right up to the last moment before printing.

The 1970s also saw the introduction and popular diffusion of video and audio recording technology. In Italy, the student movement was the first group to understand and develop independent video production. In 1972, the leftist revolutionary group *Lotta Continua* [Continuous Struggle] together with Pier Paolo Pasolini (the poet, writer and filmmaker, known outside Italy as one of the most significant directors to emerge from the second wave of Italian postwar cinema in the early 1960s) produced one of the first full-length features, *October*, shot entirely using video equipment. Thanks to spontaneous groups of militant videomakers, video cameras began to appear at political street demonstrations. In 1970, Alberto Grifi, a Roman director who came from the 1960s' performance art movement, produced a full-length video entitled *Anna*, one of the first videos to connect performance art and political information in a TV-movie format. In these years, Grifi produced an enormous number of videos documenting the political and social struggles of the student and workers' movements, inaugurating a poetics of fragmentation that borrowed heavily from the aesthetics of the beatnik movement.

New media producers were recruited out of the students and blue-collar workers who made up an emerging social formation: the "proletarian youth." These men and women engaged in socially subversive actions such as squatting or the expropriation of the goods needed to survive (food staples, electricity, or heat). They took charge of the production and distribution of political tracts, documented street actions and demonstrations with video cameras, and became involved in the construction of independent (and illegal) radio stations. Thanks to this structural transformation in communicative production, Italy in the 1970s—which for various political and social reasons enjoyed a clear lead over other European countries in this field—experienced a merger between artistic experimentation and subversive political intentions, which was similar to the experiments of the American counterculture of the 1960s, albeit in a different social and political context.

Radio Alice

The battle for democracy in the global infosphere took different paths according to the particular situations and histories of different countries. For instance, while in the United States the main danger to the freedom of communication came from privatization and foreclosure of access, in Italy the principal danger came from the public monopoly of the airwaves. During the postwar decades, European governments did not grant access to the airwaves to any private citizen—not for any purposes, commercial or political or cultural. As we saw in chapter 1, in Italy, the monopoly of the airwaves was broken in December 1974, when the *Corte di Cassazione* [Constitutional Court] declared the state monopoly over communication to be unconstitutional.

Even before the Court's decision, a collective called Controradio was formed in Bologna to evaluate the consequences of violating the law on broadcasting and opening a radio station, which was to be called Radio Alice. This initiative was shaped by the editorial board of *A/Traverso*, a local magazine concerned with issues related to the techno-scientific and theoretical knowledge of communication from below. This magazine was directly inspired by the artistic avant-garde movements (dada, futurism, surrealism), by rock and pre-punk countercultures, by mass media studies (from the Frankfurt School to McLuhan) and by the West Coast psychedelic vision of media as vehicles for human interaction.

Radio Alice connected these different strands and translated them into a media activism that spoke the sophisticated language of French poststructuralism. In the 1970s, philosophical thought, particularly in France, reopened the reflection on power and liberation in terms of microphysics, that is, in terms of power relations through which molecular social processes operate at the level of interaction between society and the social imaginary. Subjectivity was no longer identified in the monolithic form of ideology, politics and social affiliation, but was found in a whole microphysics of need, imagination and desire. The idea of social "microphysics" was introduced by Michel Foucault (1972 [1969]) and then developed in Deleuze and Guattari's *Anti-Oedipus* (1977 [1972]). In this book, the concept of the subject was substituted by that of "subjectivation," in order to suggest that the subject is not pre-made, socially determined and ideologically solid. Rather, in the formation of social subjectivities, we must see how the processes of attraction and fantasy model individual bodies and collective organisms and render them dynamic, variable and proliferating subjects. Foucault's *Madness and Civilization* (1965 [1961]) and *Discipline and Punishment* (1977 [1975]), *Anti-Oedipus* by Deleuze and Guattari, and *A Lover's Discourse* by Roland Barthes (1978 [1977]) were books that generated a keen interest in Italy during those years. Even though they did not propose a political program, these books ended up becoming reference points for the political discussions of the time. These books proposed a nomadic style that was nonidentitarian, flexible, creative and noncompetitive. The Bolognese movement in general, and Radio Alice in particular, took its language and behavior from these books, and as a result promoted the social movement as a symbolic agent and the media production collective as, to quote Felix Guattari, a "collective subject of signification."

Founded by a small group of young men (in the words of a local feminist, "by a group of all men who walked arm in arm and spoke nonstop"), Radio Alice was an island of male self-consciousness operating in a context in which women were reasserting their specificity and autonomy. It is not possible to understand this experience without realizing the impact of the feminist critiques on male protagonism, power relations and leadership ambitions. The choice of Lewis Carroll's fictional heroine was pointed; Alice was heavily linked to the world of feminine symbolism but also to the upside-down logic of *Alice in Wonderland* and *Through the Looking Glass*. Next to Carroll, as a second godfather, the group elected the Deleuze of *The Logic of Sense* (1990 [1969]), a book which deciphered the paradoxes encountered by Carroll's heroine as a metaphor for the mechanisms of loss of identity (for Deleuze, Alice wanted to always be outside all logic, and the mirror—as symbol of identity—had to be continually crossed over). The radio collective promoted an environment that discouraged the petty drives of identity, such as runaway ambition and shameless self-promotion, in favor of a truly collective voice.

The feminist movement was decisive in the redefinition of cultural and political programs for the Italian social movements. Radio Alice emerged from the awareness that the historical actor was not a unitary and homogeneous social class, but a storm of singularities that expressed themselves on different levels, such as those of sexuality and language. For the first time in Italy, sexuality and drugs became subjects of discussion and experimentation. Radio Alice was the explicit and declared signal of the desire of the new social movement to break out of the linguistic schemes of the traditional workers movement and to propose new agit-prop techniques: mockery, irony, the spreading of fake news, the mixing of lyrical and hysterical tones, and the mixture of the historical reflection with ordinary events of everyday life.

The relationship between social processes and technological change was at the center of the theoretical preoccupations of the radio collective. Radio Alice tried to recast the connection between technology and social effects of communication in a new light. In the socialist theoretical tradition, communication was seen as a superstructure where systems of ideological content clashed and fought one another, true information against false. For this reason, the strategy of the historical socialist movement was to contrast the dominant sources of news with a counterinformation capable of recovering hidden or manipulated truths. It wanted to contest the consensus around the dominant information by means of propaganda and counterinformation, and to build an alternative consensus around progressive or revolutionary ideology. Marxist schools of thought conceived cultural and communicative production as part of the superstructure, an effect determined by the relations of production. So communication was considered (in accordance with the tenets of historical materialism) in purely instrumental terms, in terms of counterinformation for the establishment of proletarian truth against bourgeois lies.

In the 1970s, French poststructuralist theory put this material vision into crisis, particularly with the publication of Jean Baudrillard's essay "Requiem for the Media" in *Toward a Critique of the Political Economy of the Sign* (1981 [1972]). The title is somewhat ironic, for Baudrillard was only beginning to develop a social theory in which the media will play crucial roles in constituting a new postmodernity. Baudrillard was really writing a requiem here for a 'Marxist theory of the media.' As an example of the failure of Marxian categories to provide an adequate theory of the media, Baudrillard criticizes the German activist and writer Hans Magnus Enzensberger's media theory and his attempts to develop a socialist strategy for the media. For Enzensberger, the political task of a socialist strategy in the field of communication consisted in reaffirming the use value of the process of signification and in organizing and setting it against the domination of capital. Baudrillard dug deeper, recognizing that the process of commodification involves the very structure of the message and the means of its production. Baudrillard took up McLuhan's essential lesson (even while raising some polemical objections): the organizational, technological and relational structure of the medium decisively influences the mode of communication and the conditions in which the communicative exchange unfolds. Therefore, the medium influences, even if in a non-determinist manner, the message itself. Baudrillard showed that the effect of communication on society depends to a substantial extent on the modalities of relation that the technology puts at the disposition of the players in the game, and not only on the ideological or political intentions of social actors.

In Italy, poststructuralist thought aroused great interest, especially in the milieus of the social movement that had been formed outside of the old militant structures of the Left. The deconstructive lessons of Derrida, Foucault, Deleuze and Guattari, as well the semiology of Umberto Eco, were strongly identifiable within the theory and practice of the social communication movement. Culture and communication were no longer regarded as superstructure, but as symbolic production related to the shaping of the social imaginary, that is—to the ocean of images, feelings, expectations, desires and motivations through which social meanings were produced and reproduced. Shaped by French poststructuralism, both *A/Traverso* and Radio Alice conducted an intense battle against historical materialism, dialectical rationality and the bureaucratic language of the socialist movements. In particular, Radio Alice's experience represented a process of appropriation of communications technologies for the creation of a new public space autonomous from both state monopoly and private economic domination.

While the Italian Left (parliamentary or not) focused only on the content of information and the development of so-called counterinformation, the Radio Alice collective abandoned this tradition to shift to guerilla-warfare-inspired informational practices aimed at permeating the whole cycle of media production. A new wave of communications workers began to understand that the real battle was not over content and social consensus, but rather over the creation of new technologies, interfaces and social linkages. They realized that it was not a matter of recovering revolutionary truth against bourgeois lies, nor about producing counterinformation to unmask the hidden plots of some enemy. It was about acting on the social imaginary, circulating plays of fantasy and flows of desire capable of destabilizing the dominant message of work, order and discipline. As an editorial in *A/Traverso* put it, it was about moving away from "consumption toward the critical production of the given and said."

Radio Alice began broadcasting on February 9, 1976, with an extended schedule (in the morning from 6:30 until 8:30 and then from 2:00 p.m. until 2:00 a.m.). The first morning, a soft female voice spoke against a background of Indian music, bidding the listeners good day and inviting them to stay in bed: "This is an invitation not to get up this morning, to stay in bed with someone, to make musical instruments and war machines for yourself." (This odd inclusion of the "war machine" was a clear homage to Deleuze and Guattari's "nomadic war machine," which will find its way into the pages of *Nomadology: The War Machine*, 1986 [1980]).

From the beginning, Radio Alice refused to be identified as an instrument of counterinformation. In the first place, Radio Alice was not a tool; it was a communicative agent. It was not in the service of the proletariat, but a subjectivity in a movement whose purpose was not the recovery of truths that had been denied, hidden, violated or suppressed. The purpose of independent communication was no longer a search for an objective truth, corresponding to the deep dynamics of history, but rather the construction of a process of autonomous expression, capable of confronting, entangling and contaminating other meaning-producing processes.

In Radio Alice's guerilla-warfare-style communication, it was necessary to appropriate the means and disturb the circulation of information, to destroy the relationship between broadcast and circulation, to dissolve the rigid division between listeners and producers. From this perspective, news had to be produced in a collective manner. The fundamental element of this tactic was the refusal of news or information produced outside the processes of the social movements—a refusal, that is, to imitate the practices of the press agencies, which hoarded news so as to insert it into a capitalist profit cycle. Everything that went on air (music, news, interviews, debates) had to be considered common property. Above all, this was true for the music choices, which were left to the personal taste (and financial means) of each participant. Everyone brought her own records (apart from one member who worked in a music shop and borrowed stuff from the store) and played her own stuff while broadcasting, and then took them away again. It was an archaic file-sharing system, an analog precursor to Napster.

Radio Alice rejected any form of professionalism as well as the division between "journalists" and "users." It was against prepared speeches, carefully produced programming and perfect mixes: "We will not professionalize. We refuse to educate ourselves. We will not learn. We don't even know what 'professionalism' means," they wrote in *A/Traverso*. Their refusal of professionalism allowed direct links with the listeners; anyone could collaborate in the making of the broadcasts.

The telephone played a fundamental role in the communicative routines Radio Alice developed in order to give listeners access to the radio. During Radio Alice's live broadcasts, the radio and telephone found themselves interacting in an increasingly intricate way. In this coupling of radio and telephone, Radio Alice produced a revolution in journalistic language that would then be imitated by many Italian communications producers. There were two innovative features: first, live broadcast of news provided reportage at the same time as the event described (most of the time through people calling in from the streets); and second, the lack of centralized coordination of this instantaneous journalism, where the radio acted as an open channel for anyone who wanted to take the podium (a strategy that we will see again with indymedia.org). In this way, the distinction between the production of news by an editorial group and its passive reception by the listener was erased. News was provided live by whoever called the radio, without any filter or editing. Freedom of access, the informal style of communication, refusal of professionalism and the live broadcast allowed the wall between broadcasters and receivers to be torn down and for the concept of private property in intellectual labor to be overcome. Every social subject became a producer of radio culture.

Opening up the radio broadcast brought with it a radical transformation of the communications context: "Radio Alice broadcasts everything: all that you want and what you don't want," its producers announced, "what you think and that which you think you think, especially if you come here in the heart of Bologna and say it on air or call us at 27 41 28." Given that all calls were broadcast live, one could sometimes hear voices that insulted the producers. One caller decried, "Filthy communists, we'll make you pay dearly for this radio station, we know who you are." Most of the time, the calls had a surrealist quality:

Alice: Hello?.... Hi, this is Alice.
Caller: Yes, what's new?
Alice: What do you mean what's new? You tell me, you called.
Caller: Exactly, what's new?

For the students and workers who were its audience, Radio Alice was "the appropriate instrument to explore the country behind the looking glass, and to intervene creatively in everyday life" (A/Traverso). Wonderland, indeed.

The radio collective sought to get rid of the distinction between technicians and producers and to avoid internal hierarchies. And even if this desire for an open and nonhierarchical project ran the danger of swamping editorial creativity with the banality of thousands of callers (a problem not dissimilar to the one experienced by Indymedia much later), at the same time, it permitted the radio to tap directly into the most creative productions of the social movements of those years. The total absence of control over access to the transmission channels allowed the spreading of every conceivable topic or theme:

Radio Alice transmits: music, news, blossoming gardens, rants, inventions, discoveries, recipes, horoscopes, magic potions, love, war bulletins, photographs, messages, massages, lies (A/Traverso).

There was bit of everything in the radio program: bulletins on social protests in the schools, discussions about sex, advice on food, different types of music, interviews with Bolognese workers on strike, travel tales, philosophy and fiction readings, cinema schedules, personal messages. One person announced: "Someone stole my bicycle, can I say on the radio that they're a son of a bitch?" The street price of drugs was broadcast, as were the results of research done on the Bolognese dialect. The established order usually given to political news and disasters by the television disappeared, while first-person accounts, freewheeling stories, local news and snatches of everyday life were given top priority.

The Revolution will not be Televised, but we will use the Radio

Radio Alice was far more than an avant-garde artistic-communicative experiment. Through its interaction with the city, it produced networks of friendships and social aggregation. For instance, one evening in 1977, someone from the radio collective came up with the idea to organize a party in the town square at midnight of the same day. With just a couple hours notice, two thousand people met in the square, "armed with milk, guitars, flutes, kites and flags for a night of improvised jam sessions and dance" (A/Traverso). At the end of the party, a cheerful and noisy march snaked through the city's streets in the deep of night, waking people and trying to convince them not to go to work the next day. Finally, it reached the door of the radio station. Only then did it dissolve into hugs and kisses.

The youth began to carry little portable radios so they could listen to Radio Alice as they moved around Bologna. If they needed to communicate something to the radio they just jumped into the first available telephone booth. Most of the time they just wanted to relate an amusing incident, get in touch with a friend, or request a specific song. However, with the intensification of the student struggles in 1977, the radio assumed a role of great political significance. It came to be used to warn students of the presence of an undercover police unit or a group of fascist thugs in front of a school, to remind people to take part in an assembly called for that evening, and to discuss strategies for fighting the city and the university administrations. Radio Alice swam in the movement like a fish in a river, a movement that until then had the levity of a peaceful cultural revolution.

Then, the March riots broke out. On March 13, during the student occupation of the University of Bologna to protest against reform proposals stemming from the "historic compromise"—the Catho-Communist alliance between the Christian Democrats and the PCI—Francesco Lorusso, a student at the University's medical school, was shot dead by the *Carabinieri* [Italian military police]. This precipitated furious clashes between youth and the police, not only in Bologna but in other major cities. Hundreds of thousands of people all over Italy went into the streets to protest police brutality and the repressive tendencies of both the PCI and the Interior Minister, Christian Democrat Francesco Cossiga (who would later become President of the Republic).

The situation became so serious in Bologna that armored tanks were sent into the streets to restore order. The students reacted by using Radio Alice to gather valuable intelligence on the police's positions and movements. During these days in March, Radio Alice became a tool for real-time communication of the complex dynamics that were occurring in the streets. It enabled those fighting the police to keep in touch in situations that were not always ideal (because of poor visibility created by tear gas, the noise of police sirens and the need to disperse quickly in the myriad small streets of the city center). Radio Alice became a collective mobile phone. The radio-telephone hybrid also provided the possibility of live accounts during the riots. The calls, broadcast live, alternated with long musical interludes and the commentary of the radio anchor, creating an audio tapestry where multiple radio genres blended in a continuous mix of voices, screams, music and excited statements.

During three days of riots between students and the police, Radio Alice fulfilled three important functions: it allowed listeners to keep abreast of events by functioning as a relay switchboard for the clashes going on in the streets; it provided a space for discussing how to respond to the police's intervention; and it injected its own perspective as a militant radio station.

Radio Alice as a Relay Station

News of Lorusso's death was conveyed live on the radio by an eyewitness just minutes after the incident:

Alice: Now let's hear from someone who is calling us from the area of the ri-

ots... just a minute, there's some confusion... yes, go ahead.
Caller: I saw a Carabiniere who jumped down and fired, I don't know if it was him, I can't say. When it happened I was there with two others, we called for help to carry him away... when I saw him he was still breathing. We lifted up his jacket and he was bleeding, they told us to hold up his head otherwise the blood would go the other way but he started bleeding from the mouth, so we laid him down on the ground and called, called, called for an ambulance. One person was so overwhelmed that he began to weep.... I immediately called for an ambulance because it seemed too serious to call a car and bring him to a sympathetic doctor. But the ambulance took ages because the police kept charging nearby and the streets were filled with teargas... at that point two ambulances arrived... he lay on the ground for four minutes, while we tried to put our hands on his brow and so on, every once in a while he seemed to be still alive, but at a certain moment I'm afraid that... that he died... I touched his forehead, it was warm... but his hands were very cold....

As soon as the news of the shooting spread, thousands of students met in the University area to express their rage:

Caller: Here I am again, sorry I'm a touch disorganized, I'm rather shaken.... The comrades in Piazza Verdi have torn up the cobblestone pavement in front of the theater next to University Hall. Lots of them have their backpacks full of stones, there are piles of them at street corners and everyone who passes by puts a couple in their pockets and then heads off quickly. Everywhere the feeling is that of rage, of determination. Tables have been taken out of the faculty buildings, as well as chairs and who knows what else to make barricades, so the area is blocked off in every direction with barricades.

Then the students decided to take the riots outside of the University quarters, and to wreak havoc on the city. At different points, participants took a break to call the radio station:

Caller: It started with a huge assembly that totally filled the square and overflowed in the streets nearby. Then we moved on, a line of locked ranks; we came from the University area and passed through Piazza Maggiore. Afterwards the demonstration continued and came upon the police, who started throwing shock-grenades and tear gas. I also heard gunshots. The riot is now full-on, and you can't see anything because of the thickness of the smoke that now rises and hides everything on the street from view.

Some calls provided a lyrical intensity until then unknown on state radio, always too concerned to separate news and commentary, a division that struck Radio Alice as absurd:

Caller: I'm coming now from the area around the train station. We made a trip by car to the crossroads of Via Marconi and Via Ugo Bassi. There are still remnants of smoke, the eyes may water a little. There are traces of the clashes everywhere, firemen are putting out the last flames, and there are lots of people talking and discussing. On every face there is a look of amazement and rage about what has happened. One still can't understand the meaning of what has taken place. However it's a fact that Via Ugo Bassi is really beautiful. It's filled with debris, the plants that decorated the arcades under which there were the finest and most expensive shops, well those plants have been torn up and wrecked. The vases have been smashed and thrown into the middle of the street. There are lots of broken windows and burnt-out shops. The comrades' rage is quite visible. Via Ugo Bassi is fantastic.

Conscious of the gravity of the situation, Radio Alice maintained a tone that was serious and informative but also capable of grasping the inevitable ironies of the moment:

Caller: Down there the fires go on, but things are not very clear.
Alice: Fire? What's on fire?
Caller: The entire barricade in front of Piazza Verdi is burning. However, the police have now stopped firing tear gas. The comrades have learned how to throw them back perfectly, and send them behind the cops. There is also a breeze that blows the tear gas back towards the police, in fact we have the breeze at our backs, there is beautiful sunshine and the air is sweet and very fresh....
Alice: Ah, wonderful, it's springtime!

This tone, oscillating between informative seriousness and the typical irony of the avant-garde's language of those years, was picked up by various callers:

Caller: About a half hour ago, around 4 p.m., we met a group of firemen wearing uniforms, helmets, oxygen tanks, etc., who were running away along Via Zamboni in the middle of the smoke from the tear gas. They said that the police cut their water supply and now they can't put out the fires anymore. That's what I heard with my little blue ears.

Faced with increasingly heavy guerilla warfare, Radio Alice continuously reported the events, relaying everything the callers said, even if potentially damaging to the students' side, such as when a caller reported hearing shots coming from both sides:

Caller: So this is the situation in Piazza Verde, the police have managed to occupy it, the comrades are dug in behind the barricade in front of the Humanities building, as well as behind the University cafeteria. There... aaah... they are

firing gunshots from both sides... throwing tear-gas grenades... at head height. That's the situation as far as we know....
Alice: Sorry, I didn't hear you there... you speak of firearms from both sides in what sense?
Caller: That is, they're firing from both sides.
Alice: Hmmm.
Caller: Or at least one can hear pistol shots from both sides, explosions of Molotov cocktails coming from our side, or something like that.
Alice: Yes.

Bologna was engulfed in a day of chaotic guerilla warfare, and Radio broadcast the rage of the student movement:

Caller: I've just slipped through the police lines. Now that the tear gas and smoke are gone people have started coming back. You can already hear their angry shouts. One more thing, all the comrades should hit the street, this is guerilla warfare, for God's sake, get into the streets.

Radio Alice and Community Relations

The radio's direct involvement in chronicling the events also produced some protests and comments from listeners, proving that the radio broadcasts were followed not only by members of the student movement, but also by ordinary citizens. Thus multiple, and sometimes antagonistic voices, were broadcast:

Caller: I want to congratulate the guy who characterized the policemen as pigs.
Alice: Right, yeah, that's me.
Caller: Well done. Now, let me tell you that you're extremely uncouth because on the radio, or TV, you don't insult people, understand? Among other things, you also cursed.
Alice: Yeah, yeah, right now who gives a fuck. I mean, these people continue to call us bad-mannered because we insult and curse on the radio, while outside on the street they're shooting us. I'll just go change the music.

Other voices from this progressive city were more sympathetic but still critical:

Caller: But listen, don't you realize that you're just stirring up trouble nonstop? You're providing no service to the community, you're continually reporting that there are clashes occurring and thus making them worse.
Alice: We do nothing but give out what we get. We're not doing the reporting, the people who are calling in are, the people who are living it.
Caller: What do you want to achieve? What use do you believe this has? What service are you providing? Please answer me.

Alice: This is just the news, and it makes itself.
Caller: This isn't news for me, it's a chain reaction. These words immediately become events. This seesaw of music, shouts, silences and dramatic facts strikes me as very kitsch.

Radio Alice let everybody speak, but also kept its own position quite clear:

Caller: It would be important for the students to go the assembly taking place right now at the psychiatric hospital and discuss all their problems, because I think they should distance themselves both from the cops who are shooting and the small bands of extremists who are fucking shit up. If they don't do so, their position is contradictory. That's what I wanted to say.
Alice: Basically, you want to invite the students to keep discussing among themselves....
Caller: It strikes me that the problems are dragging on, and the students have to bring their answers to the discussion.
Alice: Okay, look, there's a situation here, maybe you haven't really grasped what's happening. There are people injured, others have been brought to the hospital and we don't know how it'll work out, so I don't know what to say to you, just that we have to keep the telephone line free.
Caller: But the students are the main players who right now have to go everywhere to explain themselves to the people.
Alice: Listen, you talk about players, I don't know, but I'm extremely agitated and confused right now.
Caller: In my opinion you should never lose your clear-headedness....
Alice: Yes, in fact I totally agree, let's not lose clarity, but I—they are taking action, right now, do you understand? We are with those comrades who are taking action, revolting, rioting, we're not interested in getting lost in discourses like yours, getting lost in bullshit.

Radio Alice as a Militant Participant

From the last comment, we can see that Alice did not shy away from taking a position and from seeking an active role in determining the events played out in the streets. It is fairly clear that Radio Alice was used by the students during the clashes, and the radio station itself was inclined to increase its own visibility by advising people to keep listening to find out police movements and where to go.

Alice: All those listening are invited to go to Piazza Verdi, to answer in person as to what has happened. Wherever possible, organize groups of listeners, always have somebody listening and call us with any news.

For their own part, the students in the streets were very conscious of the role that the radio was performing:

Caller: We need information for the comrades, so that they know... they are calling the radio station and there is always someone here listening to the radio. There is a need to know because we need to organize ourselves with barricades and so on.
Alice: Yes.
Caller: We need to know if there are cops at Porta Zamboni, if they're on Via Irinerio, if they're at the circle behind the Hall of Anatomy... I mean, what's it called? Well, whatever, in the ring around Porta Zamboni.

Some correspondents seemed conscious of the possibly negative consequences (both legal and intelligence-wise) of providing live information:

Caller: Listen, um, maybe, I don't know how to say it.... I need to ask if it's possible to get more comrades.
Alice: Yes.
Caller: That is to support us, because it's not as if there are hordes of us.
Alice: Yeah, we heard you.
Caller: Okay?
Alice: Thanks, bye.
Caller: Fine, bye. Maybe if there is news later I'll call back with it.
Alice: Okay.
Caller: Okay, or maybe someone else will, bye.
Alice: Bye, thanks.

In the heat of the riots, the radio station's efforts were concentrated on providing detailed information to the students in the street about the police's movements and possible exit routes:

Alice: Listen, do you know if... if there's a way out there on Via San Donato? If there's—
Caller: A way out through San Donato? Not really.
Alice: Basically—
Caller: Via Zamboni is blocked.
Alice: All blocked.
Caller: Also you can't go through the ring.
Alice: Is the demonstration there?
Caller: Nope, no demonstration.
Alice: Where are the comrades?
Caller: The comrades are in the little streets behind Piazza Verdi, but lots of them are here in the University, in assemblies, because the meeting with the journalists has just finished.
Alice: Okay.
Caller: Listen, there's an open corridor through Piazza Roosevelt and the little square beside it.

Alice: Okay, very well.

Radio Alice didn't limit itself to passing on the word; in some cases it was clearly involved by callers in the elaboration of strategy for the course of the riots:

Caller: So we're here in Via Zamboni, the police still haven't managed to get past the barricade... the majority of the comrades at Porta Zamboni are... it doesn't matter, they are undecided whether to disperse and reconvene in Piazza Maggiore or to go to Via San Donato. But I think that they'll probably break up and go to Piazza Maggiore. If you have any ideas, say them before we finish up so that I can go tell them.
Alice: Let me talk with the people here—listen to the radio.

Later in the day, once the riots subsided and the students returned to the University quarter, Alice became the promoter of the multiple assemblies organized to discuss how to proceed in the next days:

Alice: We'll continue to broadcast, don't despair. We'll go on transmitting whatever fragmentary news we have. Now there's massive confusion. Outside it's beginning to rain, if I'm not mistaken. The general assembly for tonight at nine in Humanities Hall is confirmed. There are already lots of comrades in Piazza Verdi with their dark jackets waiting for it to begin. The assembly will start at 9 p.m. Lots of people are already there, others are arriving. I think it's really important to participate... not just for the exchange of information, but also to decide how to continue. These have been incredible hours, after the murder of this afternoon. His name was Francesco, a medical student.

Radio Alice's role as media protagonist thus became a fundamental element in the synergy between radio and movement, so much so that it became impossible to distinguish between the voices of the radio station and the callers, which merged into a choral "we":

Alice: Let's remember that for every incident that has occurred, incidents which the state television drew attention to tonight, such as the fires, the destruction of the newspaper office, the burning of two police stations, the attack on the Fiat office, all these things, like the clashes that happened at the train station, all the comrades assume full responsibility for them. Everyone took part in this enormous collective effort; we prepared our Molotov cocktails together in the square, everyone ripped up the pavement to get stones, everyone had incendiary devices in their hands and bangers in their pockets, because what happened today was a violent demonstration decided on by everyone, because this was the only way to stay alive.

Radio Alice acting as a protagonist did not please the police, and in the middle of the night on March 12, the police stormed the station, stopped its transmission, and blocked its frequency.

Alice 2: So the police come and then what? Leave the mic on, as high as it can go.

Alice 3: Don't run away, calm down.

Alice 1: If there's a lawyer out there... if there's a Legal Defense Collective lawyer out there, please come here immediately, please, immediately. The police are here right now, aiming their pistols and submachine guns at us. Everyone, everyone listening, the police are here wearing bullet-proof vests.

Alice 3: Calm down, guys, calm down. They're coming in now, take this away.

Alice 2: Do they have a warrant?

[Police heard at the door.]

Police: YES!

Alice 2: Should I come out?

[Police heard shouting. Phone rings.]

Alice 1: Alice? Please hang up, the police are here.

Alice 4: What? Are we going to get on the roof? From there?

Alice 3: Calm down guys.

Alice 2: Don't open the door, don't open it until someone comes.

[Phone rings.]

Alice 2: Hello, Alice. Yes? Listen, the police are here. If you can find someone from the Legal Defense Collective... send them here immediately.

[Sounds of objects being moved around.]

Alice 2: Take this thing here. Don't escape out the window.

Alice 1: No, I don't give a crap, listen, it's more important... yes, listen, put it down, please, come on. Attention, attention all lawyers, all comrades who are listening to us, please contact the lawyers immediately. Attention all comrades, all comrades who are listening right now, please try to reach Attorney Insolera or anyone from the Legal Defense Collective.

Police: ALICE?

Alice 4: I'll shoot at them, I'll shoot.

Alice 1: Daniela, if you're by the phone, I mean, if you're by the radio, be calm.

Alice 3: No, where are you going?

Alice 2: Give me the phone number. Does this one work? This one here, Gamberini 51?

Alice 4: The house?

Alice 3: Yes. 51 80 66.

Alice 1: Again, a plea from Radio Alice. Radio Alice has the police at the door. Please, our comrades from the Legal Defense Collective, please hurry here, we're in Via Pratello.

Alice 2: Is anyone answering?

Alice 3: No one's answering.

Alice 1: Attention, attention. All comrades from the Legal Defense Collective, please call the radio station, please come here immediately.

[Phone rings.]

Alice 2: Hello? Yes? It's Mauro. Listen, the police are here. We're waiting for the lawyers.

Alice 1: Attention, Radio Alice is still here. We're still waiting for the lawyers to arrive to let the police in. The police are trying to break down the door right now. Put that thing down.

[Phone rings.]

Alice 2: Hello? Who's there? Yes, the police are outside, trying to knock down the door. They have their guns drawn and I'm refusing to open the door. I've told them I won't do it until they put down their guns and show me their warrant, and since they aren't putting their guns down, I told them we won't open up until our lawyer arrives. Can you please come here? Right away, right away please. These assholes have guns and bullet-proof vests. Via Pratello 41, okay? We're waiting for you, bye.

Alice 3: Tell him—Mauro, be quiet.

Alice 2: The lawyers are coming. Just a minute, the lawyers are coming.

[Phone rings.]

Alice 4: The phone, the phone.

[Police heard shouting.]

Alice 2: After the lawyers get here.

Alice 4: The phone.

Alice 3: Alice.

Alice 4: God, this sucks.

Alice 3: Listen, we have the police here, hang up please.

Alice 2: Attention, Alice is still here. We have the police outside the door. We have the police outside the door. And—we have the police outside the door with bullet-proof vests, guns drawn and the like, and we're waiting for our lawyers. We're refusing to let the police in before the lawyers get here, and because they have their guns drawn and such, and these are things we absolutely cannot accept, and [laughs] okay. Please, Radio Città comrades, if you are retransmitting this as I believe you are, please give us a sign through the radio, I'm listening to you.

[Radio noises.]

Alice 3: Before midnight, absolutely. Radio Città, please call Radio Alice.

[Phone rings.]

Alice 3: Hello?

Alice 2: Radio Città, please call Radio Alice. Radio Città, please call Radio Alice. Or let us know you are listening and retransmitting this thing over the radio. Please, we're listening for you, but we can't tell whether it's our return or if it's their retransmission. Please, Radio Città, please let us know.

Alice 3: Thanks.

Alice 2: Radio Città try—friends of Radio Città, call your comrades. In any case, comrades, the situation is under control.
[Phone rings.]
Alice 3: Hello? Ma'am, we're just waiting for the lawyers.
Alice 2: The police are... situation under control. The police are still outside, waiting to come in, still in their bullet-proof vests with guns drawn. They've said they are going to break down the door, and we ask all comrades who know lawyers to call them, and tell them that we are under siege by the police right now, just like, I don't know if you've seen the movie, what the hell was it called? [Laughs.] The one by Boelkorff in Germany, about the Katherina Bloom case. The same exact elements, the same—bullet-proof vests, guns drawn, stuff like that. It's truly absurd, truly incredible, truly [laughs] like a movie. I swear that if they weren't breaking down the door, I'd think I was at the cinema.
[Phone rings.]
Alice 3: I don't have it here. Listen, does anyone know the number for Radio Città?
Alice 1: 3 4 6 4 5 8
Alice 3: 3 4 6 4 5 8
Alice 2: We're still waiting for our comrades to arrive.
Alice 3: Bye, thanks.
Alice 2: There's four of us here at the station, and... nothing... there are four of us doing the work of counterinformation, and we're waiting to see what the hell the police do. For the moment, they seem calm, there aren't making so much noise. They've calmed down, they've stopped banging on the door. You can tell they think it's really strong [laughs].
Alice 2: Give me a record, I'll put on some music for Christ's sake.
[Phone rings.]
Alice 3: Alice?
Alice 2: The phone here is always ringing, really always ringing. Here's some Beethoven, if that's okay, if not, tough shit....
Alice 3: Hello? No, Calimero left. Yes.
Alice 4: My God, I knew it, I knew it would happen.
Alice 3: No, listen, listen. We have the police outside who are....
[Music in the background.]
Alice 2: A bit of background music.
Alice 3: I don't know, listen. I don't know if I'm going to sleep at home to-night.
Alice 4: Go tell them we are waiting for the lawyers.
Police: OPEN UP!
Alice 2: Now the police have started banging on the door again. They're shouting for us to open up. Look alive, get down.
[Shouts from the police.]
Alice 4: Our lawyers are on the way, wait five minutes. Eh, they're here on the street.

[More shouts from the police.]
Alice 2: Their only comments are for Christ's sake open up, things like that.
[Phone rings.]
Alice 2: Alice? I don't know who Alberto is. Anyway—eh? No, this isn't Matteo, listen, the police are at the door.
Alice 3: They're in.
Alice 2: They're here. They've come in, they've come in.
Alice 3: They're here, they're here.
Alice 2: They've come in, they've come in, we have our hands up. They've come in, we have our hands up.
Alice 3: Look, they're taking off my mic.
Alice 2: They're taking off my mic. We have our hands up, they say that this is a place of....

The Radio Alice collective was later indicted for seditious activities and many of its collaborators were imprisoned.

Two days later, Radio Alice started broadcasting again using borrowed equipment and on a different frequency, but by then Bologna was under curfew and the police were searching many houses, seeking any media activists involved with the radio station. Many of them elected to leave Italy, temporarily or for good, rather than face a biased prosecution. The political spring of 1977 had come to an end.

Coda: On Forgetting and Technological Obsolescence

Rather than an appendix to the proletarian struggles of the twentieth century, or the tail end of the student movements of 1968, the revolt of 1977 anticipated the political and communicative dynamic developed in the following two decades. The proliferation of communication tools was central to the youth revolt of 1977. In the following years, however, technology developed rapidly: formats and standards changed in the space of just a few years, rendering the equipment used by the first wave of media activists obsolete. The field of video production is a good example. Between 1976 and 1979, hundreds of videomakers with ties to the social movement used Beta video cameras to document everything being produced at that time: ordinary life, political events, ludic plays and the many public performances of the movement. When more advanced technologies became available (Super-8, Hi-8), they adopted them. It was only many years later that they realized that the rapid obsolescence of standards and deterioration of the electronic storage media had rendered most of the products of the work of those years unusable. With many media activists outside of the country, Beta videocassettes and audiotapes of radio recordings were left to rot in cellars for years and years, decaying past the point of recovery, and thus sinking those years of electronic experimentation into the distant past, as if buried under centuries of dust and forgetfulness. Between 1976 and 1979, Radio Alice produced hundreds of audiocassettes and scores of videotapes, but few documents have perservered. The material quoted above was saved, ironically, by the

Italian police, who had requisitioned it after the break-in on March 12, 1977 and archived it as evidence for the trial against its producers.

The following account from a member of Radio Alice's staff, however, allows us to see in this unpredictability and obsolescence much more than an inevitable material condition of those years, but rather an echo of things to come:

> One night I was doing a program about Mayakovsky, in a totally casual way. It was three o'clock in the morning and I received a phone call. Calls at such an hour were rare and the noise made me jump. We talked live, she told me that she was a stewardess and this made me think that she must be pretty. I had the impression of a certain excitement in her voice, knowing that she was being broadcast all over Bologna, in the middle of the night. At the end she asked to meet me and added, "Let's meet, but let's not see each others' faces." I agreed. "Come to my house," she said, "I'll keep it dark." I went to her house on my bicycle. The door was left ajar. I entered in darkness. Suddenly I felt her presence, she reached for my arm and took me to her room, her voice no longer warped by the technological medium. We talked for ages, lying stretched out in the dark, her face still a mystery. She was a good talker but a little strange, because she would intentionally mispronounce some adjectives. She said many times that she was tired (mispronouncing that word) but then continued to talk in her funny way. She was a young woman, I could tell from her voice. The mood was very ambiguous. Then she said to me, "If you want, you can sleep here, but I don't want you to come close." I said, "Okay, no problem." We slept there together. When I woke up in the morning she wasn't there. She had already left. I never saw her face. This is my favorite metaphor for that period. It was a time full of enthusiasms, excitements, passions, impossible expectations. And then it all just vanished. Just like her that night.

four

Internet Activism and Post-Mass-Media Culture

After the spring of 1977, Italian media activism skipped summer and went straight into a long winter, which lasted well into the 1990s, when the rise of Berlusconi's media power and the parallel emergence of new communication technologies (above all the Internet) produced new conditions for mobilization and dissent. The story of Italian media activism in the 1990s must be framed within the general context of the conflict between a videocratic system—in which power structures of finance, advertising and television converge—and the horizontal network of media democracy. In the mediascape of this decade, two contrasting tendencies were intertwined: a) the formation of an interconnected "global mind," wired according to the lines of semiocapitalist power; and b) the formation of a resistant "collective intelligence," capable not only of autonomy and self-determination, but also of forwarding different priorities than those of the capitalist economy.

The battle between these two forces shaping the mediascape started in the 1990s and still rages on, using digital communication as their weapon of choice. The choice of the Internet as the site for battle can be traced to its rhizomatic agency and to its acentric, diffuse and nonhierarchical nature. This meets the needs for the self-organization of cognitive work according to an egalitarian and diffusive process. In the course of the 1990s, several large companies, above all Microsoft, attempted to colonize the Internet through the imposition of standards subject to proprietary control. Thanks to the simplification of research and connection procedures, this colonization project was able to infiltrate the working modalities and cognitive models of the Internet. But despite these attempts at colonization, cyberspace did not cease to proliferate in unforeseen and uncontrolled directions: ever-more innovative content was produced, ever-more sophisticated interfaces were experimented with, and programs that evaded proprietary control and the free market model were created.

While Microsoft attempted to enclose the Internet, at its margins, patrols of experimenters sought escape from this control by using open source technologies, providing free access to data and programs, and producing collaboratively. This has enabled the subtraction of a large part of the cognitive workers of the Internet from the economic and imaginative domination of semiocapital. In the 1990s, the multiform practices of net culture spread like wildfire, creating conditions for a mass critique of media. For the global revolt begun in Seattle in November 1999, the Internet served not only as an organizational and informational tool, but also—and above all—as the formative space for a reclaimed public sphere, an energized social imagination and innovative production models. Notwithstanding the colonizing actions launched by the large software companies, the Internet continues to function as an organizational tool for the international cognitariat who continues to perform their role in gathering and spreading content, and even succeeding in several cases, as in the days of revolt in Seattle, in exerting a genuine net-culture hegemony over the global media system.

The crisis that struck the entire information economy at the turn of the millennium has initiated a new phase that may have unpredictable results. In the years of dotcom mania, financial capital and advertising had a determining influence on the creative work of the majority of netizens. But during the economic crisis, financial investments in, and advertising on, the Internet declined drastically. This certainly had an impoverishing effect, which, in the long run anyway, might subtract productive energies from the domination of capitalist culture.

Aside from the incursions (as invasive as they might be) of advertising, up until the end of the 1990s, the flow of communication on the Internet was for the most part self-regulated and self-produced, working toward the social, cognitive and imaginative interests of the men and women who used, frequented and nourished it. During the boom, the economic interest in the Internet had created a dangerous commercial regimentation and generalized homogenization of content. The economic crisis reduced the involvement of the large financial and advertising groups, and for a brief moment, restored the possibility of independent production.

The boom and crisis of information economy produced new social scenarios and new possibilities for media activism, and in this chapter we would like to first address the transformations of the world's social imaginary as a result of new information technologies, and then look at various Italian cases of digital media activism.

The First Video-Electronic Generation

In 1984, in a book entitled *Mind and Media: The Effects of Television, Video Games, and Computers*, psychologist Patricia Marks Greenfield reported an experiment performed in a Canadian city in the 1970s in which researchers were able to follow the behavior of a certain number of children before, during and after the spread of television sets in their community. The findings indicated that the creative imagination of these children tended to decline when television came to occupy the principal spot in the mediascape. However, together with this atrophy of the imaginative ability, members of the first video-electronic generation acquired new competencies: they were able to read and orient themselves in a highly complex semiotic universe, they acquired executive skills of ever more complex semiotic manipulation, and they were increasingly at ease with multitasking.

So far however, nobody has looked at the sociopolitical effects of the intense mobilization of semiconscious attention by the extremely complex and interconnected media system that has developed in the last three decades. How does the collective mind react to the increase in infospheric pressure, to the acceleration of stimuli, to the intensification of production rhythms? Cognitive ability, intelligence, attention and imagination are put to work, subsumed within the process of the development of capital, and thus subject to the intensification of productivity, to constant acceleration, competition, the rules of victory and defeat, failure and aggressiveness. Social attention is constantly mobilized, both from the point of view of production and from the point of view of consumption. Many of the production processes of high technology, in fact, require time and attention. Attention must also be constantly mobilized to consume: the semioproducts that constitute a large part of contemporary consumption require mental time and attention, uninterrupted mobilization of the cognitive faculties.

In 1977, anthropologist and mass mediologist Rose Goldsen wrote in the foreword of her book *The Show and Tell Machine*:

A generation ago, people in this country began to watch images of wrestlers, trained poodles, and pitchmen on television sets placed mainly in public places such as bars and store windows. Today the television set, standard equipment in the American home, so blurs the distinction between the public environment and the privacy of the family that it is ever present even as the tiniest babies are ushered into the social system. Human beings whose primal impressions come from a machine—it's the first time in human history that this has occurred. What such an innovation might mean for the way the human consciousness develops, quite apart from the content of the materials the machine transmits, nobody yet knows (1977: iv).

When Goldsen was writing that book, a new generation was beginning to form itself in front of the television. Now the first video-electronic generation is reaching adulthood. Again, more than a social change, we find ourselves in front of a cognitive change, a change in the psychic, cognitive and linguistic makeup of humanity.

Western people who grew up in the 1970s and later have gained a breadth of abilities that do not have precedents in the history of the human mind: they have acquired the ability to move themselves rapidly through a universe chock-full of electronic visual signs. Their ability to read images has developed at a skyrocketing pace, and this ability holds an important function among the skills of semiconscious formation of a contemporary individual. The problem posed is not that of judging the cognitive skills of the new generation, but of interpreting them. Whoever intends to communicate with the new video-electronic generation must remember how the collective postliterate brain works, keeping in mind McLuhan's warning, according to which mythic thought tends to take precedence in cultural formation over logical-critical thought.

It is difficult not to believe that the speed at which the mind is exposed to video-electronic messages is a cause of increasing volatility of attention. Under the extreme speed of video-electronic inputs, the mind is briefly engaged, then tends to quickly move away, to seek another object. Rapid transfer proceeds by association—by substituting critical understanding with correlations. Never in the history of human evolution has the human mind been subject to such an intense and invasive bombardment of sensory information. Whoever is around children in a teaching capacity knows that in the last generation, the concentration time of children on a mental object has continually decreased. Now, it is difficult to hold the attention of a boy or a girl on an object for more than a few seconds. As a result, in the United States alone around five million children take a psychopharmaceutical drug called Ritalin that is used to treat so-called Attention Deficit Disorder.

Nicholas Mirzoeff writes in his book on visual culture: "Western culture has consistently privileged the spoken word as the highest form of intellectual prac-tice and has seen visual representations as a second-rate illustration of ideas" (1999: 6). Instead, the language in which the global imaginary expresses itself is that of visual culture. Cultural globalization has been able to develop much more through visual media than through the written or spoken word. Images function as activators of cognitive, behavioral and mythopoetic chains that can be generated beyond the limits of verbal language and the interpretative grids of culture, na-tion and religion. Visual language is therefore the *lingua franca* of the first video-electronic generation, a generation that has learned more from the television set than from mom and dad, in the sense that a significant part of its emotional and cognitive imprinting depends more on the exposure to the mechanized semiosis of the television or the Internet than it does on its relationship with parents or with other human beings.

Should we consider the first video-electronic generation to be emotional mutants? While social communication is ever-more mediated by technological systems, and the presence of bodies in social space becomes ever more superfluous to the ends of the exchange of messages and interaction, it seems as if the forms of unmediated communication lose coherence and efficacy: attention deficit hyperactivity disorder, aphasia and dyslexia spread into the behavior of individuals, and psychopharma-ceuticals become an increasingly indispensable support for a socialization that has become weak, asphyxiated and anorexic.

Media Culture and The Crisis of Universal Humanist Values

Since the early part of the twentieth century, the birth and development of electronic media has constituted a critical element for political democracy and for critical and progressive thought. Since the first developments in radiophony and cinematography, critical thought has taken an ambivalent position regarding electronic media, a stance which is entirely understandable. Already in the interwar period, Benjamin and Adorno had outlined two different critical intellectual sensibilities regarding the diffusion of mass media. Benjamin intuited that the technical reproduction of messages creates completely new conditions of aesthetic perception and communication, while Adorno presented a humanist and elitist vision that saw in mass communication a state of decline in the artistic and cultural arena.

But it was Marshall McLuhan who made the change in the rules of the game clear. When the simultaneous succeeds the sequential, when electronic technology succeeds literacy technology, at that point, discursive communication forms cede the way to forms of configurational communication, and mythic thought tends to prevail over forms of logical-critical thought. This is the reason why, in the last decades of the twentieth century, the political culture of the Left was revealed to be inadequate to seize the new possibilities of media, and has remained at the margins of the grand transformation that brought electronic media to the center of social communication. The political Left was formed on the values of critical thought, and it has kept at the center of its own intellectual panorama the dialogic value of democracy. The Left has not been able to gracefully free itself of the idea that social communication is composed primarily of dialogic and discursive acts, directed toward the acquisition of a rational and critical consensus. This has prevented it from accepting the brutal transformation of the scene that has made the 'mythic imaginary' the privileged field of social communication and of public opinion formation. The Right, indifferent to the values of criticism and democratic dialectic, has known how to seize the mythologization of the social field, the passage from the discursive field to the imaginary one that has been verified by public opinion, and thus has known how to reap the greatest advantage from the mediatization of social communications.

The choice presented to progressively inspired critical thought derived from humanism is a painful one: suffer a definitive marginalization in mass culture due to emerging forms of the neomythic imaginary, or react in the name of humanist values that electronic media tend to cancel out in the perception of the great majority of society. It is a complicated situation, because critical thought is forced to choose between an implicitly conservative position and one of subordination to the cultural models that are affirmed in the hyperspectacular infosphere. As the experience of the last twenty years teaches us, in this situation, politically progressive critical thought finds itself in a defensive position facing the aggressive exuberance of the neomythic culture of the Right and the breakout of identity-based cultural forms that recall the aggressive values of belonging rather than those of universalism.

In this difficult situation, humanist thought foreshadows the appeal of the eruption of media cultures, and simultaneously reports the dangers to democracy that are implicit in this change that involves both the mediascape and the collective mind.

TV Meets Web

In 1990, George Gilder published the book *Life After Television,* in which he outlined the prospective transformation of the television system. The agent of this transformation, according to Gilder, would be digital technology, the computer and above all, the Internet, which in the early 1990s was heading toward a mass explosion. There was great activity surrounding this project, a visionary spirit that pushed many scholars to imagine the future of the Internet in terms of the expansion of its borders and of the convergence of diverse media within one reticulated system. The endpoint of the transformation would be, according to the hypothesis of Gilder, the 'telecomputer,' namely a television set designed to function as a computer connected to the Internet.

> Tired of watching TV? With artful programming of telecomputers, you could spend a day interacting on the screen with Henry Kissinger, Kim Basinger, or Billy Graham. Celebrities could produce and sell their own software or make themselves available for two-way personal video communication. You could take a fully interactive course in physics or computer science with the world's most exciting professors, who respond to your questions and let you move at your own learning speed. You could have a fully interactive workday without commuting to the office or run a global corporation without ever getting on a plane.
>
> You could watch your child play baseball at a high school across the country, view the Super Bowl from any point in the stadium that you choose, or soar above the basket with Michael Jordan. You could fly an airplane over the Alps or climb Mount Everest—all on a powerful high-resolution display (1990: 40–41).

Notwithstanding the optimism for the future that fourteen years later seems rather annoying, this passage outlines the concept of convergence between television and the Web.

The techno-communicative model of television as we have known it from past decades is oriented toward broadcast, to the diffusion of a single flow of visual information coming from a single source and directed toward a receiving public that is unified and passive.

The techno-communicative model of the Internet is oriented toward networking, namely toward a plurality of visual information flows coming from multiple sources and directed at restricted sections of a public which is differentiated and capable of interaction.

When we speak of convergence, we do not speak merely of the broadening (no matter how boundless) of the spectrum of available television stations thanks to digital reception technologies such as the parabolic antenna, cable or satellite. We speak of a new concept of production and consumption of the televised image. As Paul Levinson noted, the new information technology doesn't necessarily displace the old so much as it expands it:

> TV, with the important exception of home video recorders, is completely pro-grammed by people other than the viewer. Computers, with the important ex-ception of the structure imposed by underlying programs such as word pro-cessing and Web hypertext, is programmed only by the proximate user. But note that the content of word processing is supplied solely by the user, and the content of hypertext is for the most part supplied by other people simi-lar to the user—in contrast to TV programming, almost all of which is sup-plied by professional TV producers, filmmakers, TV network programmers, and so forth.... Each TV station broadcasts exactly the same programming to everyone.... Television is, to a significant degree, an "incidental" medium in its condition of attendance—meaning that people can do other things when the television is on.... TV screens for the most part traffic in images and sounds, with occasional written words. Computer screens, as we have explored in de-tail, traffic in text, with occasional (but increasing) presences of icons, images and sounds (1997: 163).

Levinson goes on to observe that the VCR has created the conditions for a transi-tion that the Internet has begun to bring to fruition. The purchasers of video record-ing devices began to record images and to acquire competence in recording and edit-ing techniques. By the mid-1990s, some even began to find themselves in a position to transform themselves into disseminated producers of television transmitted via the Web.

At the end of the 1990s, several large groups involved in the field of television and the computer industry began to use the Internet as their main production vehicle. In July 1996, MSNBC, a joint venture of Microsoft and NBC that put news and television reports at the disposal of Web users, began operations. In the same period, CNN also put some of its television reports online.

The creation of an online television system also required several technological preconditions, such as the digitization of television products. A large part of the investments made in the early 1990s in high-definition TV (HDTV) ended up going in this direction. Investments in HDTV projects allowed television to proceed along the road of digitization and contributed to the convergence of television and the Internet, which by the end of the 1990s became an actuality.

If we want to reconstruct the process of convergence, we must not only the course taken by the large telecommunication companies or the products destined for mass consumption. We must also keep in mind the 'disseminated panopticon,' namely the proliferation of webcams and the experimentation of various forms of techno-art. In the process of convergence, indeed, we must not only look at the technical problem of unified support, but on a cultural level, the mobilization of as producers.

Let us glance at the world of webcams. This expression refers to a flow of images recorded by video cameras placed anywhere in the world, controlled by a person or left on without control, and received by a server in order to be passed onto the World Wide Web. Any Internet user can connect to the address corresponding to the webcam and receive the images (in continuous movement, immobile or in sequence).

There are people who show the deserted landscape of their surroundings, or girls who show their legs, or youth who are stunned in front of the lens, or simple automated broadcasts of city intersections (as Andy Warhol did more than thirty years ago, when he installed his movie camera in front of the Empire State Building for twenty-four consecutive hours).

Omnipresent, interconnected electronic eyes, open to record a frame of the universe and to make its viewing available almost anywhere in the universe.

The Aleph of Borges in Progressive Realization

Webcams represent the nucleus of a process that finds its horizon in the tendency that we will call 'hypermedial convergence.' A particular argument should also be made regarding artistic experimentations and performances that have been multiplying all over the world. Artists have entered the field of linked technologies by experimenting with languages appropriate for diverse and innovative platforms, such as online video.

At the San Francisco Museum of Modern Art in 1998, Julia Scher (USA) distributed television monitors throughout the rooms and corridors of the building and these terminals transmitted images simultaneously recorded in other corridors and rooms of the same building. The spectator thus got used to seeing normal museum scenes, such as people who walk around slowly and stop to look at this or that. However, from time to time, unpredictable images casually appeared on the screens, such as the image of two completely nude young men running through one of the rooms. Real time constituted a communicative dimension in which it was possible to introduce unpredictable and bewildering breaks.

Other artists have tried to hint at a new perception of geographic space in their performances. Felix Stefan Huber (Switzerland) and Philip Pocock (Canada) have installed a parabolic antenna on a van that, traveling from Alaska, Klondike and Dempster Highways to the edge of the Arctic Sea, sent daily messages and video clips to their website, thus connecting Arctic space with virtual space. In the spring of 1999, Andrea Renzini (Italy) held a performance that took place physically in Marrakech, but that could be attended in real time via the Internet by an audience at a gallery in Bologna. Experiments of this type are multiplying, often with scarce attention to the image quality, because the problem is entirely conceptual.

The essential part of the prediction that Gilder advanced in his book went on to come true in the following years, even if many details did not follow directly along the lines he imagined. Since Gilder wrote his book, it is common knowledge that the passage from analog to digital television involves not only technology, but also economics and culture. The multiplication of channels is in fact destined to bring enormous masses of the public away from the generalized flow and toward an ever-greater fragmentation of offerings, and consequently, the offering will need to adapt itself to this change. But it is not enough to speak of a channel revolution if we are not able to speak of the revolution related to content. There cannot be any revolution in content if it does not pass through a reformulation of the relationship between the flow of images and the communications system; between the transmitter and the territory.

The broadcast audience is being progressively eroded in favor of a narrowcast audience, something already foreseen by Gilder in 1990. But we should go beyond this simple distributional fact, we should deepen the relationship between the techno-media system and the social connections that it makes possible.

The number of spectators will be the same, but they will be able to choose between a myriad of different possibilities. If, however, these thousands of possibilities are all culturally and socially homogenized, if they are simple clones of a subaltern advertising image, then the multiplication of channels will not serve any purpose at all except to increase disorientation.

The point of departure for Gilder's reasoning was a prediction about technology: the diffusion of broadband owing to the use of fiber optics. Today, thanks to the increase in capacity and management of this infrastructure, it is possible to begin to conceptualize an integration between the Internet and the production and diffusion of video, beyond the horizon of what we know as 'television system.'

Television has always been a centralized communicative system. The relationship model between transmitter and receiver has always been unidirectional with the passivizing effect on the receiver-telespectator. Furthermore, the costs of production for television have always prevented access by those who do not have large amounts of capital at their disposal to invest and are not able to gather advertising revenue. It has always been this way, but today this is no longer true. The means of visual production have become accessible: a collective, a social center, an artist or a group of independent artists can easily afford a digital video camera.

The digitization of visual production machines has allowed for the immediate integration of the visual product with the Internet. At this point, streaming video has only taken its first steps. Thanks to the growing availability of broadband, it is now possible to circulate large quantities of streaming video over the Internet. It is also possible to create banks of visual data, genuine jukeboxes, accessible by internauts (who remain for the moment a tiny minority of the world population) and by tiny television stations that can transmit content via the Internet to the household TV set. What is emerging now is the possibility of a new integration between the Internet and recombinations of fragments of visual production.

Media Convergence and the Danger of the Colonization of the Internet

The convergence that emerged at the turn of the millennium is an important aspect of the autonomous operation that cognitive workers have been developing at the technological level and in their ventures into new media systems. It indicates the tendency for flows of audio, video and text to meld inside the multimedia Internet. In the process of convergence we have seen many opportunities but also many dangers. At the beginning of 2000, at the culmination of the economic boom—and exactly on the eve of a steep decline in stocks on Wall Street that marked the definitive reversal of the stock market trend—the merger between America Online and Time Warner appeared as the signal of an imminent infiltration of the Internet by entertainment and advertising giants. The netizens went into a state of alarm. A month after the WTO protests in Seattle, Time Warner was moving toward the conquest of the Internet, using the largest existing provider, America Online, as its Trojan horse. The convergence of Internet service provider and television content provider represented a drastic change in the Internet's communication model.

The goal seemed clear. HyperTV intended to swallow the Internet, to subtract the production of content from individuals and groups that willingly and knowingly joined together in the infosphere, and to transform the Internet into a replica of the television model: homogenized signals for a homogenized public, programs produced according to the interests of a very small minority, for the taste of the majority, pushing the users to consume the Internet as they consumed television. If this design had been fully realized, it would have meant the colonization of the Internet by television; the invasion of the Internet by the semiotic flow of homogenized entertainment. But things did not go this way. The crash of Nasdaq a few months before the merger of the two giants resulted in confusion and disinvestment. Media convergence under the power of Microsoft and AOL-Time Warner did not occur.

The corporate colonization of cyberspace has continued, but it has never fully succeeded in absorbing all the energies and attention of Internet users. So far, the convergence model has produced unforeseeable results. On the one hand, control of the Internet by large economic and media groups has increased. At the dawn of the Broadband Age, the flow of traffic on the World Wide Web began to resemble that of commercial television. In its first five years of existence, when the Internet was growing exponentially, diversity prevailed. But by 1999, according to Jupiter Media Matrix, 110 global companies controlled 60 percent of the connection time of users. Only two years later, this number was reduced to only 14 companies. By 2004, with the growing dominance of AOL-Time Warner and Microsoft, the model of democracy that the Internet appeared to be was becoming an oligarchy. The broadening of use did not correspond to a greater variety of information offered because new users tended to follow ever-more uniform navigational paths.

At the same time, the innovations launched by base groups or by net artists set in motion avant-garde social experiments that changed the workings of entire zones of the Internet. A tidal wave of international media activism could redefine the entire mediascape. Media activism has its origins in the mass diffusion of tools for video recording, editing and image transmission. A vast number of sites made streaming video possible, resulting in the invasion and disturbance of television space. The most significant phenomenon in this field was certainly indymedia.org, the largest, best-constructed and most democratic environment for world social movements. The very existence of Indymedia and the principle of radical self-organization on which it was developed, constitutes the emergence of a form of information, coordination and production that is both global and local.

Indymediea.org, also known as the Independent Media Center, was born during the Seattle revolt, when a loose federation of independent media (radio stations, local television stations, photographers and journalists of various mastheads) came together to cover the events.

From that point on, Indymedia proliferated, thanks to the formation of local branches in each country—and occasionally in every city—that put online information about the global movement against corporations. It is a question of a diffusive communications experience: democratic, acentric and at the same time working toward a common operation; toward the formation of a global community that is not limited to protest nor to the exchange of information, but constructs zones of autonomous existence from the rules of capital.

Indymedia represents an easily exportable model from the terrain of textual information to that of visual information. It has put streaming video at the disposal of user-participants to document the history of the movement. Now, the Indymedia model can converge with the model of webcast stations, and make navigational interfaces available between all producers of images who want to renounce the exclusive rights to their products.

The latest generation of activists, many of whom emerged from the WTO protest in Seattle, has given life to the global network of the anti-corporate movement, developing a practice suited to new media and elaborating a media theory that takes into account the potentialities and dangers implicit in new communication technologies. It is not our intention to reconstruct the history of media activism, but we must point out some of the experimental forms of media production that grew from the 1980s to the 1990s in America as in Europe: Paper Tiger Television (PTTV) in New York, Van Gogh TV in Hamburg and Candida TV in Rome all underscore the fact that the critique of television had a long incubation.

Social and Ideological Effects of the Dotcom Economy

In the 1990s, telecommunication of the Internet became the main support for mass capitalism during the long expansive phase of the dotcom boom. Tens of millions of people invested their money without leaving their homes, buying and selling stocks from their online positions. Today that long phase of expansion has entered into crisis, and the Internet, fantastical multiplier of popular participation in the market, risks becoming the multiplier of its crises, and the vanishing point for the system of media-financial control.

Thanks to mass participation in financial investing in the 1990s, cognitive workers self-organized and invested their competence, knowledge and creativity in the dotcom arena, and financed their businesses using the stock market. For several years, this undertaking forged a meeting point between financial capital and cognitive work, giving rise to a form of production that exalted the autonomy of work and at the same time, dependence on the market. The neoliberal model adapted itself perfectly to this process, and American cyberculture provided the ideological background (even founding its evangelist in the magazine *Wired*). But this digital-liberalist *Weltanschauung*, disdainful and triumphalist, collapsed in the first two years of the new millennium, along with the new economy and most of the army of self-employed thinkers who had animated the dotcom world.

It failed because the model of a perfectly free market is a practical and theoretical falsehood. What neoliberal ideology has favored in the long term is not the free market, but the monopoly. And while the market was idealized as the free place in which various expertises, competences and creativities interacted, reality demonstrated that large controlling companies did not act at all in a libertarian manner, and imposed themselves with force (of media or of money), and shamelessly pillaged the common shareholders and the cognitive workforce. The falsehood of the free market came to light with the first Bush presidency. The politics of this administration explicitly favored monopolies (beginning with the scandalous acquittal of Bill Gates, in exchange for a political-economic alliance). With Bush's victory in 2000, the neolibertarian and laissez-faire ideology was defeated, and it became a hypocritical repetition of commonplaces without content or truth. The same thing occurred in Italy. Berlusconi presented himself as the champion of neoliberalism against state control and governmental intervention as represented by the Left. But behind the market ideology he was busy establishing a monopoly for himself, a monopoly that used the power of government and the law to sanction corruption. Italian neoliberalism was nothing more than an ideological smokescreen behind which took place classical power grabbing of public resources and unchecked business arrogance.

In the years of dotcom boom, a provisional and fragile alliance came about between cognitive labor and capital financing. But when that economic tide ebbed with the dotcom bust, cognitive work found itself cut off from capital. Digital artisans, who in the 1990s felt themselves to be owners of their own work, began to feel they had been cheated. They bitterly realized that even though they possessed all of the production power, they had been robbed of the fruits of their labor by a minority of ignorant speculators who had nonetheless managed the legal and financial aspects of the production process. The unproductive part of the virtual class, the lawyers and accountants, had appropriated the cognitive surplus generated by the physicists, computer scientists, chemists, writers and media operators.

This situation could produce a new consciousness for these cyber-operators, so that they can separate themselves from the judicial and financial fortress of semio-capitalism and construct a direct relationship with users. Only then will the process of autonomous self-organization of cognitive work begin. This process may already be underway, as the experiences of media activism demonstrate.

The struggle between media activism and videocracy in Italy can be read in this context. The Berlusconi regime prospered during the period in which neoliberal ideology had a solid base of consensus. But after the dotcom crash and the resulting economic recession, a growing divide emerged between the interests of the dominant group and those of the cognitive workers upon which the functioning of the communications system was based. The sectors of innovative work that participated in the illusion of the new economy and mass capitalism in the 1990s were precisely those that, in the new decade, were most exposed to the crisis. Fortunately, a number of cognitive workers and the most dynamic strata of the high-technology workforce managed to turn their situation of weakness and isolation into self-governance. Media activism emerged as the expression of the disconnection of the techno-media system from social consciousness and cognitive work. It gave voice to the autonomous transformation of the social communication system. In fact, the change of technologies made independent production and communicative connections possible, and since the dotcom crash cognitive workers have begun to assume political, cultural and scientific responsibilities, actively intervening in these technological transformations instead of passively suffering their effects.

Media activism is a conscious function of the technological and communicative change that developed in the last few years, at the intersection between diverse media languages and the global paradigm of the Internet. One must keep in mind the problematic field tied to the prospects of open source technology, free software and computer hacking, because these have been the first manifestations of autonomous appropriation of the technology system by cognitive workers. Media activism is an aspect of this autonomous reappropriation of competencies and technologies.

Subvertising

The linguistic masterpiece of capital is advertising: a flow of pronouncements unchained from any pretext of truth, and precisely for this reason capable of making suggestions, constructing fictional worlds, capturing social desire, then mobilizing and exploiting it. Advertising gives voice to feelings, provokes emotions, prompts unconscious identifications and bends them in pursuit of an objective that at one level is commercial and on a deeper level is ideological or anthropological. The user of advertising language (the consumer) is not so ingenuous as to believe the literal truth of the content of the message. He knows full well that the advertiser is playing and creating simulations of the world in order to induce the consumer to identify with a made-up character, in order to convince him to buy a certain aftershave rather than a competing product. Beyond its banal commercial solicitations, advertising seeks to sell a product bigger than all products, namely the context in which all products become goods: capitalism. A large computer company launched a laptop with the image of a young man who was happily waterskiing with the computer on his knees. The slogan enthusiastically exclaimed: "At work everywhere." In essence, the ad proposed a lifestyle in which workers are flexible and available twenty-four hours a day, always giving their work and their time, always participating in the uninterrupted cycle of producing surplus value.

In the battle of social communication, a soldier advances who does not use the weapons of the reasonable opposition or the instruments of counterculture, but fights madness with madness, suggestion with suggestion, falsity with creative falsification. This soldier is a media activist who uses the weapons of subverted advertising, and for this reason he has been dubbed a "subvertiser": a semiotic guerilla fighter who has developed over the course of the entire twentieth century, and who comes into complete form in the time of generalized advertising communication.

Subvertising has been consciously theorized by the Canadian journal *Adbusters* since 1989, and is a reference point for all who want to use linguistic techniques of advertising to reverse the function of advertising communication. In effect, linguistic saboteurs have been firing their ordinance at the fortified castles of the powerful in the communications sphere for decades, indeed for an entire century. Dada, Surrealism, the Beat Generation, the Situationists and Mao Dada transversalism were all experiments in linguistic sabotage. Subvertising begins when it is intuited that it is possible to slyly usurp the pronouncer's power, showing his distinctive signs and speaking in his tone of voice, to make him say things that destroy his authority. Subvertising consists of pushing the falsification of power to the limit, to reveal its weakness, its unbelievability, its madness.

"False information produces real events," claimed the Italian magazine *A/traverso*, which launched campaigns of info-subversion in the 1970s. Communication sabotage groups were born all over Italy at this time. In Bologna, fake copies of the local conservative newspaper *Il Resto del Carlino* exclaimed: "This year, as always, there have been thousands of work-related deaths. Thousands of Bolognese wipe their asses with *Il Resto del Carlino*." In Naples, a manifesto was posted that carried the stamp and the letterhead of the Prefecture, inviting the population to come to the supermarkets and take goods without paying. In 1978, this same group created the tabloid *Il Male*, a satirical newspaper that occasionally simulated the mastheads of major Italian newspapers to announce impossible news such as the landing of Martians in the Piazza del Duomo, FIFA's decision to cancel the results of the soccer World Cup (which Italy lost in the finals), or the arrest of actor/director Ugo Tognazzi as the head of the left-wing terrorist group, the Red Brigades.

Protest movements all over the world have used falsification to creatively detourn messages of power, and in recent years, communications-based sabotage operations have multiplied, thanks to groups that work over the Internet such as rtMark, and groups linked to the circuit of Indymedia or *Adbusters*. Subvertising has only taken its first steps, and has yet to construct an exact science of creative falsification.

Convergence and Postmedia Culture

The process of convergence for postmedia culture has followed contradictory tendencies. In the spring of 2000, it was thought that the convergence might be dominated by economic investments of television infotainment and advertising culture giants, and there would be no space left for cultural experimentation and social self-organization. Despite the process of economic concentration of information that has continued to grow as the use of the Internet expands, the convergence still contains unpredictable possibilities. The framework of the Internet is very complex. Economic concentration constitutes the dominant quantitative trend, but this does not limit the proliferation of agents of individual and collective transmission who make use of the Internet's global diffusion and intermedia intersections.

On the theoretical level, this prospect was foreseen by Felix Guattari in the 1980s with his concept of a postmedia society. In those years, as the power of new media began to emerge, and in Italy, Big Brother assumed the televisual features of Silvio Berlusconi, the theoretical imagination was paralyzed by the danger of an absolute dominance of the media by economic power. In this atmosphere of medialogic pessimism, Guattari, with his schizoprophetic gifts, spoke of the possibility of a postmedia society. Exactly while the mass media system was becoming the central agent of cognitive colonization and political authoritarianism, Guattari was saying that one need not fear the dominance of television over the flow of social communication: the progress of computer technology would soon make a vast diffusion of rhizomatic devices possible. "There will be bidirectional and multidimensional relationships between collectives of postmedia transmission," he said. These devices and their relational models would infect the centralized television system, disturbing and destructuring all state-controlled and hierarchical economic forms.

Clearly Guattari was predicting the utopia of the Internet, the ever-proliferating rhizome of brains and machines. This utopia is incarnated within technology, in culture, even in enterprise. But like all utopias it is not pacific, and within the emerging postmedia society it has presaged an inevitable war—the recurrent and interminable war between domination and liberty. The 1990s saw the rise of the rhizomatic communicative system, but this system quickly became infected by centralizing and hierarchal media viruses. The penetration of the Internet by advertising, business and television represented an aspect of this infiltration. The imposition of proprietary software was another aspect. But the complexity of the rhizomatic system was no longer reducible in any significant manner to a totalizing and centralized project. Following this logic, Guattari's post-mass-media prophecy seems to be incessantly belied and reaffirmed by the dynamic of domination and freedom.

But there is a more radical aspect of this post-mass-media prophecy. The fundamental question that we must pose is: to what extent does mediatization involve, disturb, repress and cancel our bodily singularity? While technologies make a growing mediatization of social interactions possible, and thus tend to promote long-distance communication and the abolition of personal contact and corporeal presence, new energies capable of recontextualizing corporeality, presence and erotic physicality are also activated. These energies occasionally manifest themselves in cultural behaviors of a Luddite nature, such as the refusal of technological prostheses and the search for an unmediated relationship with nature. Occasionally, they manifest themselves through the refinement of a visionary-futurist style that proposes to bring the energy that comes from psychedelic creativity into the media infosphere.

On one hand we must ask ourselves what direction mediatization is taking us, which tendencies will predominate in the mass media universe or which force will predominate in the process of convergence; on the other, we cannot fail to ask ourselves about our corporeality in relation to the diffusion of cyberspace. We are caught in this conundrum because our virtual communicative lives make an expansion of our experience possible, but at the same time continually threatens to paralyze us, and to destroy our singular sensibility.

One of the fundamental struggles of the present epoch is the continual reactualization of the singular sensibility of our existence in both real and virtual dimensions. This is what Guattari defines as the 'post-mass-media battle.'

five

Telestreet: The Archipelago of Ethereal Shadows

Throughout this book, we have discussed the futility of opposing Berlusconi's media takeover. Within this situation of powerlessness, however, a new type of phenomenon spread at the margins of the official media system: Telestreet, a network of micro-television stations using a low-power signal to broadcast over a very limited geographical area, sometimes a single street (thus the name "Telestreet" or street televisions). These micro-television stations transmitted via the ether, utilizing so-called "shadow cones"—areas where the signals of commercial terrestrial broadcasters could not reach because of natural or trade barriers. This movement of "antennas toward people" aimed to enable citizens to freely use the communication channel of television to not only to receive information but especially to produce it. By doing so, it allowed individuals to closely interact from a distance in sharing and co-producing information. "Don't watch TV, just do it!" was the slogan of the street televisions.

The very low cost of the equipment gave everyone the opportunity to transmit information not typically covered by mainstream networks. Moreover, antenna broadcasting was combined with the Internet, allowing video works to be shared and aiding in the management of the street televisions scattered all over Italy. A new Italian media activism had emerged within protests organized around the Social Forums, and found itself not only capturing the events, but also propagating an atmosphere, an impatience, a desire for autonomy.

OrfeoTV

The first Italian micro-television was created in the first months of 2002 by a group of people who had lived the experience of free radio twenty-five years before, namely Radio Alice. The group included several media professionals, transmission technology experts, an antennist and a computer programmer. This heterogeneous little group circulated the following message on some Italian media activist sites like ECN, Indymedia and Rekombinant:

> Let's go down into the street, let's get together our friends, life-long companions, those 'still-alive,' who still have their voice and thoughts, let's buy an antenna, a frequency modulator and a TV transmitter, find a room, a garage or workshop, hook up our Sunday afternoon video camera, videocassette recorders, a television set and a couple of lamps for light. We can now begin.

People responded to the call, and during the spring of 2002, in a central district of Bologna—a city, as we have seen in the preceding chapters, with a long history of avant-garde experimentation in communications—a motley group of media activists were performing strange experiments. One person would go around on the roofs of the houses with odd devices, scanning the radio spectrum. Others would disassemble television receivers and turn them into transmitters. Still others would interview passersby. After several attempts, the group discovered a "shadow cone"—a blind spot where no transmissions are receivable for mainly topographical reasons—along the spectrum of the television frequency at channel 51 (MTV-Italy). Thus, the conditions were set for broadcasting within a radius of a few hundred meters. The group then tested the broadcast signal and success was confirmed by checking the reception of channel 51 from different houses in the vicinity: within a range of 300 meters, the signal was received very clearly.

The headquarters of the first Italian street television station were established in Mick and Max's bar on Via Orfeo, a place seemingly untouched for fifty years, through which several generations of artists and freaks had passed. The initiation of the broadcast was announced at a local street party and groups of activists with video cameras went around the neighborhood interviewing people. The group's manifesto was posted on the walls of the district:

Citizens,
The television ocean in which we are immersed is starting to seriously stink of monoculture.
Only one type of fish dominates the great waters of the infosphere.
Communications biodiversity is at risk of extinction.
The banana fish is eating all the others.
LISTEN UP, strong and free fish who still love to swim,
chase the anxiety and depression from your hearts.

Now is the time to come out of the aquarium.
Let imagination and creativity rediscover their strength,
let friendship and challenge guide us into the open,
for where there is danger there is also salvation.

A press conference was called at Mick and Max's on June 21. The summer had scarcely begun and the bar was hellishly hot. To an assemblage of overheated journalists, the group announced the launch of an Italian micro-television station called 'OrfeoTV' (taking the name from its district). The OrfeoTV antenna could only cover a radius of 300 meters, just a few buildings, a small neighborhood. The first broadcasts were dedicated to the neighborhood, including a documentary about the protest against the proposal to destroy a local park in order to build a parking lot, and profiles of local craftsmen. The broadcast ended with coverage of a massive street demonstration organized the previous week for the defense of union rights and against the policies of Berlusconi's government.

Everybody was initially swept along by the wave of media enthusiasm, but after a while, the group realized that while broadcasting an hour and a half each day was easy, preparing the material to be transmitted was not. The fact that the broadcast range was just a few hundred meters or that the audience was little more than a couple of dozen people did not make any difference. It still required the same amount of work as any television station: recording, selecting, editing and all the rest. The station used any available video camera. Someone from the collective was able to tap into the resources of a few local private television stations, and later, students from the Communications Department at the University of Bologna provided some help. Pidgin, a small video production company located in the vicinity and sympathetic to the project, provided an editing facility. But this worked for only a few weeks. The editing machines could not be permanently made available, as the editing studios had to be used for commercial jobs. Thus, whoever went out to shoot had to try to edit using the camera. In some cases, OrfeoTV even experimented with a breathtaking new editing technique, daring but efficient: the operator charged with broadcasting the recorded material decided when the piece was getting a bit boring and "cut it" by pushing the fast-forward switch during transmission.

Several viewers phoned in to complain, "I can't tune in this evening," said the woman who lived just two buildings down the road from the broadcast. Others called in to give messages of encouragement to the group.

But what mattered in terms of the objectives of the original group was not the quality of the programs or the images. At its heart, OrfeoTV was a conceptual work more than an effective television station. It was a simulation of postmediatic democracy; a symbolic protest against the media monopoly in Italy; an experiment in what one could call 'postmediatic society.'

For several weeks, OrfeoTV transmitted an hour and a half each day. Not quite enough time to say that an independent voice had come to life in the television system, but enough to demonstrate that a clandestine anti-government television station could be operative. The collective did not want this initiative to remain isolated or circumscribed by the local conditions of one district in Bologna, it believed it had to proliferate. It wanted other groups of media activists to climb on top of their roofs, find shadow cones in their neighborhoods, alter a television reception unit and begin broadcasting. But what should they transmit? Whatever made up everyday life, social struggles and cultural projects that opposed and subtracted themselves from the teledictator's show.

The OrfeoTV collective wanted to show that it was not only possible to set up a pirate television station, but also that this experience was easily replicable in any urban context. Telestreet proposed itself as a national platform for the coordination between micro-TV stations.

In a second manifesto distributed via the Internet, the OrfeoTV collective spelled out their call to all Italian media activists:

Everyone knows that in Italy we live in a televisual dictatorship.
Thanks in part to his domination of the mediascape, a scoundrel has seized political power. And thanks to this political power he can feed his media power.
There's no way out. Many fear that he is destined to rule forever.
But it's not like that. Because television is dead.
The energy of social communication is shifting in another direction. The direction is that of the Internet. But the majority of the Italian population receives most of the signals that influence its social brain from the television screen.
Thus, we must we must bring the message to that screen and connect it to the Internet.
In the immediate future, our task is to connect the circuit of audiovisual production within a territorial grid (neighborhood by neighborhood) of short-range micro-broadcasters.
And so the first thing to do is to build this grid.
We will call it Telestreet.

To answer the questions of those who wanted to know more, a website (www.telestreet.it) was launched and a mailing list was activated. Hundreds of people contacted the OrfeoTV studio to propose broadcasts of every type; everyone wanted to interview someone. The unexpected success of the initiative also had some drawbacks, including burn-out on the part of some members of the original group. "One guy came up to me the other day in the suburbs," recalled one member of the collective, "and asked me, 'This idea of Telestreet is great. I live on the tenth floor, what can I do?' I would have liked to have answered him, 'Throw yourself off your balcony,' but instead I told him, 'go and have a look at the list of technical criteria for a micro-TV station on Telestreet's website and put up your own station.'"

What is Needed to Transmit

The collective distributed a document explaining how to set up a micro-television station, what the problems were, and how they could be resolved. The document contained the following: Gather the materials technically necessary for transmission, find an unoccupied frequency in your area and get the transmitter working; we would advise you to get the help of somebody who knows TV antennas. The costs for getting a micro-TV station going are difficult to estimate. The basic technical materials don't cost much, less than a thousand Euros in all. But naturally, you need the help of technically qualified people.

In the case of OrfeoTV, such competencies existed within the collective and were volunteered to the project, but it is not a given that it will be like that for everyone. In some cases, it will be necessary to pay for assistance, and this will add to the initial costs.

The Production of the Flow of Images

The production of the broadcasts depends on your communicative and poetic intentions. There is no minimum standard in this field; everyone can broadcast as they please. The transmissions can be edited using sophisticated machines or one can forego all post-production work and live-broadcast someone reading poetry by Paul Eluard, or transmit the statements of a street's inhabitants who casually address a stationary video camera.

A list of the materials necessary for production and post-production includes: a video camera, possibly digital, a video mixer and an editing kit. Many collectives, social centers as well as amateur videomakers, possess everything necessary to make professional broadcasts. You should find people in your area, among your acquaintances, who will to allow you to achieve a decent level of production.

With regards to content, the task the founding group of OrfeoTV set for itself was to create a network of micro-TV stations throughout Italy capable of exchanging materials and knowledge over the Internet. These media activists saw the future of street TV as an integration of micro-TV stations with a global circuit of video production. Every micro-TV station would be able to access an archive of images, films, documentaries and video of every type produced by media activist collectives throughout the country. The Internet would handle the exchange between the different micro-TV stations.

In July 2002, the collective organized a meeting of media activists in Bologna to explore different possibilities for the creation of a 'jukebox' of streaming videos that would function as an open-source archive for every micro-TV station. The most brilliant hackers set to work on devising a compression system that would make an archive of image streams freely accessible to the street television network.

Someone asked: "But how is it possible to find a frequency in the overcrowded ether?" And someone else answered: "The spectrum of television frequencies is entirely occupied by the big TV operators who obtained government permits. But anyone with knowledge of TV reception knows that in urban areas there exist frequencies that, although having been assigned, do not in fact carry the signals for unpredictable geographical reasons: a hill or a building may be so high that it impedes sight to the repeater. With a small transmitter you can send a signal in a shadow cone capable of reaching the antennas that are to be found in that little area." Others asked: "Is it legal or illegal to transmit without a government permit?" "Oh, it's illegal, yes, illegal."

Of course it was illegal. The law regulating the field of television broadcasting (the so-called Mammì Law, approved in 1984 under direct pressure from Bettino Craxi) was specifically designed for Berlusconi and thus it is illegal for anyone to transmit without a government permit. The collective expected to be shut down any day.

OrfeoTV broadcast every day throughout July 2002 and nothing happened. If the authorities had decided to intervene, a fine group of Bolognese media activists would have ended up in jail. The theory that circulated was that it would have been pretty scandalous if a regime that based its power on control over the whole communications system intervened to shut down a tiny street television station broadcasting to a mere few blocks.

The Legal Question

In order to answer these legal queries, the Telestreet website opened a discussion on the legal question. First of all, let us keep in mind the fact that Article 21 of the constitution guarantees equal right of information to all citizens: "Everyone has the right to freely express their own thoughts by speech, the written word and every other means of distribution. The press cannot be subject either to censorship or the need for authorization." Secondly, let us recall that the Constitutional Court's Judgment 202 from July 1976 establishes the illegitimacy of the broadcast monopoly and at the time there was a state monopoly, in which RAI was the only body recognized by the state as having the right to send electromagnetic radio and television signals.

Following this court decision, a proliferation of free radio stations became possible. Today, that decision acquires new meaning because the monopoly has been reconstituted, even if it no longer has the features of a state monopoly. Rather, it is the monopoly of a public-private financial and political group.

During the years following 1976, private television stations began to form and as they spread, various legal problems emerged. One problem in particular concerned nationwide unified broadcasts. Legislation was passed on this issue in 1984; the Craxi government requested the drafting of an ad-hoc law explicitly devised to favor those groups intending to broadcast television nationwide (i.e., Mediaset). This law—quickly approved so as to regulate a difficult legal situation for the then-rising star of private television, the young Silvio Berlusconi—took the title "Mammì Law" from then-Minister of Communications Oscar Mammì.

This law states that private parties can transmit television only after obtaining permission from a government commission that meets every four years. Those without permission (which none of us could ever obtain, for technical, financial and political reasons quite aside from the question of overcrowding) are not allowed to transmit and do not even have the right to own equipment capable of transmitting.

The Mammì Law also states the sentence for someone who transmits or who possesses transmission equipment: nine-to-eighteen months incarceration for anyone who transmits nationally, and half of that for someone transmitting locally. Beyond this, obviously, the equipment would be confiscated.

When the collective prepared to launch OrfeoTV, its members asked themselves a thousand times: "Will they, or will they not, shut us down?" Some believed the station would be closed swiftly by administrative decision rather than for political reasons. Others believed that no one would close the station down because it would be rather embarrassing for a magistrate to order the closure of a microbroadcaster when everyone knew that Italy was governed by a bully who had taken control of 90 percent of the available ether.

Indeed, nobody came to seize OrfeoTV's equipment and no one was charged with breaking the law. If this had happened, the group was prepared: they had their lawyers ready to invoke Constitutional Court's 1976 decision, which proclaimed the illegitimacy of the monopoly; that is, the illegitimacy of the situation created in Italy after the victory of Fininvest in the elections of May 13, 2001.

Whatever may have happened, OrfeoTV would have won. If Berlusconi's regime did not close the station, it would have created a legal precedent allowing anyone who wanted to do so to create their own microantenna. If it closed the station down, the ensuing legal battle would have opened up a long-overdue debate on the state of the Italian media, and could have produced the conditions to shutdown Mediaset for clear breach of the court's ruling.

The Archipelago of the Ethereal Shadows

In the summer of 2002, the OrfeoTV collective produced a third manifesto that outlined the national project of Telestreet in broad strokes:

Orfeo is a microbroadcaster, a street television station.
Orfeo covers an area of a few hundred square meters.
Orfeo uses a broadcast power of 0.07 watts.
Orfeo does not produce electromagnetic pollution.
Orfeo was started for less than a thousand Euros.

Orfeo is the self-financed and voluntary fruit of a common sensibility in its becoming.
Orfeo knows it can be pursued legally.
Orfeo knows that it can count on Article 21 of the Constitution.
Orfeo knows how to act in a viral manner.

Orfeo transmits in Bologna on channel 51 in a shadow cone of MTV.
Orfeo does not interfere with MTV or any other broadcaster in any way.
Orfeo knows that there are thousands, tens of thousands of shadow cones.
Orfeo imagines a broadcaster in every shadow cone.

Orfeo imagines Telestreet, a national network of street television stations.

Today, Telestreet is a website whose address is: www.telestreet.it.
Telestreet gathers supporters, offers information and creates contacts.
Telestreet opens itself to the global circuit of independent video productions.

Telestreet will be the technical, political and informational platform of the street TVs.
Telestreet will be the place for the coordination and exchange between all street TVs.
Telestreet will function as a global, interdependent and interactive editorial staff.

Telstreet will accomplish the integration between micro-broadcasters and broadband Internet.
Telestreet will integrate broadband Internet with satellite TV.

The urban legend of the little pirate broadcaster opposing the huge dictatorship of the national mediascape began to circulate. Groups wanting to recreate the experience of OrfeoTV were founded in different Italian cities. The first objective of the group of media activists all over Italy who organized themselves as Telestreet was the denunciation of Berlusconi's media domination. Flyers and leaflets were distributed everywhere to promote the micro-TV philosophy against the power of the banana fish.

The Banana Fish is Poisoning Us

The banana fish has infected the aquarium and now the stench is intolerable. An economic group that built its power on illegality, the corruption of judges, and the systematic marginalization of intelligence, is poisoning thousands of hearts and minds. It is the vilest form of fascism: the dictatorship of media-produced ignorance.

The master of Mediaset has entrusted RAI to his personnel. The waiters of the man from Mediaset are cleansing the public service of every ounce of intelligence and information. From the airwaves we will only be able to get that which loyally serves the dictatorship of ignorance.

But in many districts of Italian cities a new fashion has begun to spread. In Trieste, Bologna, Rome, Florence, Termini Imerese and other places we don't even know about, groups of media activists have started creating street-TV stations. They are capturing the images and words of the people. They put up an antenna and connect it with a short-range transmitter. They broadcast daily life in the range of daily life.

OrfeoTV has been transmitting several hours each evening, two or three days a week, since June 21. Its message is: "Turn off the television of the regime, turn on the video camera, create a group of media activists who go around and do interviews, collect, mix and edit. Put up your antenna, create your own television station." It doesn't take much. You need an antennist capable of locating the blind spot for the television frequency and technical equipment costing little more than a thousand Euros. And most of all, you need the time to discuss and work together, and freedom of imagination.

A wave of neighborhood televisions can bring some oxygen to this dying country.

Telestreet is not advocating a better television, nor one that is more just or more pretty. This is the end of television, the end of this tyrannical medium you have been forced to endure. It's the beginning of a process that can spread everywhere: of seizing the word and image by a peaceful army of networked communicators.

Telestreet initiated a discussion of theoretical elaboration and practical experimentation. Other nuclei of media activists began to follow the example of OrfeoTV, to root out the blind spots in the frequency spectrum of their neighborhoods, and to build a transmitter capable of sending short-range television signals, and to record, edit and broadcast streams of information, video art and creation. It was not easy for any of these activists to build the technical instruments needed to start broadcasting, and still less so to find the time and energy necessary to activate an editorial process.

The process slowly began to spread, with the aim of bringing a network of neighborhood micro-TVs to life that would produce video information in a diffuse manner and were capable of covering—through the proliferation their short-range antennas—a growing part of the national territory.

From OrfeoTV to Telestreet

The following is an excerpt from a document that summarizes this first phase of the Telestreet experiment:

On June 21, in a neighborhood in Bologna, the first free video antenna arose: OrfeoTV.

The studios are in a tiny shop, three square meters, and the potential audience extends a few hundred meters between the Via Dei Coltelli, Via Castiglione and Via Degli Angeli.

How many viewers are there? Personally, I know three.
Maybe there are others, but we don't have Auditel.
OrfeoTV would only be a joke of questionable taste if it weren't for Telestreet.

And what is Telestreet?

1. Telestreet is a symbolic campaign against the teledictatorship. David always wins against Goliath. It takes some time but it's always going to finish that way.

2. Telestreet is a project for convergence from below: neighborhood microantennas connected via broadband networks. Only a few people are able to understand the concept today. We appeal to those few. Thanks to this concept, we will destroy television. Samson will die with the Philistines.

It is not important how many people watch and listen (television is always crap). What matters is how many people speak and record (making TV is the very opposite of being subjected to television).

Everyone should do it; this way no one will watch it anymore.

This is the principle.
This is the alpha and the omega.
This is convergence from below.

The Closing of Telefabbrica

In October, new street televisions started up in other Italian cities. One in Trieste, others in Pisa and Florence. In the autumn of 2002, Fiat, the country's main car manufacturer, went into one of its recurring catastrophic crisis. Thousands of workers were laid off at Fiat's main plant in Turin but also in Termini Imerese. Termini Imerese is a small Sicilian town that is home to a Fiat plant that is the sole source of work and income for thousands of people. Fiat's decision to close the factory meant poverty for thousands of families. Some local media activists decided to document the fight against the closure by setting up their own telestreet called Telefabbrica. A group of youngsters began to interview the laid-off workers, trade-unionists and women who were protesting. The interviews went out over the airwaves each evening. The micro-TV's office was located on the premises of the trade union and for three days television was used as a tool to discuss the problems of the workers' resistance. The military police of the Carabinieri arrived on the fourth day, seized the transmission equipment and prevented these young people from continuing their broadcasts.

Telestreet, the national coordination of street television stations, responded with the following communiqué:

Today, December 4, 2002, a group of Carabinieri, on the orders of the Minister of Communications, shut down Telefabbrica, a street TV born in Termini Imerese to support the struggle of the Fiat workers threatened with layoffs. Telefabbrica had been broadcasting since Saturday evening within a radius of five hundred meters. The Minister of Communications gave the order to close it.

Five hundred meters. This is more or less like preventing two deaf mutes from gesturing to one another from opposite sides of the road. The message sent by the government seems clear. No one has the right to communicate anymore, only He (and His orderlies) can. Telefabbrica did not have a government permit giving authorization to broadcast and therefore was in violation of Article 195 of the Mammì Law. Retequattro (one of Berlusconi's national networks that was supposed to broadcast only via cable but never complied with the order) has no permit either, and its operative radius is not five hundred meters. But Retequattro can transmit because it's the property of the dictator and thus the Minister of Communications doesn't shut it down.

Telestreet was born to raise consciousness that it is possible to break the communications monopoly simply by assuming the responsibility to communicate. By all means, including television. It's possible to do it, it costs little, and it sets creative and political energy in motion. Telestreet was born to bring democracy into communications, precisely what in this country there is an attempt to destroy.

This is why Telestreet calls on all sentient people to experience the same disgust that we feel at this comic repression that prevents people from transmitting words and images in a range of five hundred meters.

After these events, the Italian media activist milieu began to ponder the significance that this televisual experience was assuming, notwithstanding how poor and down and out it was.

For all those involved, it was clear that two different elements in the Telestreet operation needed to be distinguished from one another: the tactical and political struggle against the excessive media power of Mediaset and the Berlusconi government; and the strategic aspect involving the production of content. For the first time in Italy, media activists tried to develop an intermedia communicative model by which the Internet could absorb video production.

Eterea

On December 14, 2002, the first national meeting of street television stations was held to unite the groups inspired by OrfeoTV that were proliferating all over the country, and to deepen the political and mediatic aspects of the Telestreet project. Five hundred media activists from many different cities attended. The conference was called *Eterea* (a wordplay on *etere*, the airwaves, and *etereo*, ethereal light). What follows is the manifesto released to organize the event:

There is a heavy air about. The environment is increasingly polluted.
Not just the physical environment, cities poisoned by millions of cars, coasts devastated by seas of oil. Not just the social environment, impoverished by avarice, attacked by private interests, frightened by the inkling of an imminent economic storm.

The mental environment also, the space of communications, where the imagination, sensibility and desire are formed, is heavily polluted with fear, arrogance, economic aggressiveness, racism and hypocrisy.

In Italy, a strange fact has come to being. A private economic power has progressively taken control of the communications system and particularly television. Let's leave aside by what methods this private group took control of everything. The fact remains that thanks to its domination over the means of production of the collective mind, this economic group has conquered political power and is using it to dismantle every democratic space in the sphere of mass communications. The purging of RAI—always central to the distribution of political power—allows this private group to attain two objectives: to eliminate dissenting voices and to bring down the quality of RAI's programming, in order to eliminate it as a competitor and take a significant slice of its advertising market.

All this was foreseen, but it still does not cease to astonish observers. However, maybe it's just better to get used to the idea and think about how to dismantle this political and mental trap.

Heaviness is not fought but dissolved. Therefore, we should not become obsessed with just the idea of providing opposition. We need to find ways that circumvent, deconstruct, break up and ultimately dissolve the heaviness that weighs upon the air. What should we do in such a predicament? Protest against the arrogance of the heavies, who took control of the public entity and are now dismantling it in their own interest? Of course we must protest, but we already know that they will not listen to us. They have no time to lose, these heavies, with the time-wasting minutiae of democracy. Thanks to a media bombardment, they have stunned the people, and out of this befuddlement come opaque hopes and the necessary votes. They use these votes to get themselves what they want day after day.

So then what should we do? Demonstrate against the racist laws or the senseless rush towards war? We did, but it didn't come to much, because a diffuse climate of war, fear and persecution is useful to these heavy spirits, where everyone lays low.

So we keep on going. We will not stop protesting and demonstrating against the heaviness, but that will not be enough to dispel it.

There is something we can do, and many of us are already doing it: experimenting with democracy, assuming the responsibility to disobey and to act in an autonomous manner in the fields of communication, knowledge, technical innovation and social action.

The behavior we are proposing is utterly ethereal, a conduct composed of withdrawal, desertion and at the same time micro-interference, a continual hijacking of the flows of language and images. The heavies have built a massive machine of domination the human mind, someone must make little vessels for escape available in a thousand directions.

The Eterea conference was a huge success. For an entire day, hundreds of media activists explored the various tactics and strategies of proliferating street television, media activism and the convergence-from-below aspects of the television grid and the illegal transmission of images in the ether.

Telestreet was born out of a critique of television, with the intention of multiplying the amount of televised transmission points in order to make the television system "delirious," (thus making it explode through proliferation) and to produce a systematic, organized activity of advertising subversion. It needed to differentiate its languages, techniques and objectives in order to become a movement of creative falsification and communicative sabotage; to be able to distribute false news capable of inspiring real events.

Television in the Time of War

At the end of July 2002, the OrfeoTV collective decided to suspend broadcasting, resolving to resume it in the beginning of fall.

Fall 2002 was marked by large mobilizations against the Iraq War: the demonstration on November 9 in Florence during the European Social Forum; No War Day on December 10, with demonstrations in every city; and a gigantic demonstration on February 15, 2003 in Rome, in which close to two million people took to the streets to protest the impending war. OrfeoTV followed these activities with three or four video cameras, assembling many hours of raw footage, but the broadcasts became increasingly erratic and then stopped all together.

Is this what the collective had in mind when they came up with the idea to launch OrfeoTV? In meetings held after the closing, they easily acknowledged that they never had an actual plan. "Destroy the power of television by simulating television, by proliferating television," was the motto that emerged from their post-mortem analysis of their operation. Reviewing the content produced by OrfeoTV, the collective cannot recall anything particularly innovative that broke with existing televised schemas, or that broadened comprehension or awareness of the broadcasting machine. There was nothing that signaled a new language or a new expressive form. The novelty of Telestreet did not lie in any innovative way of producing images or creating information, or in the capacity to enter into unknown places or discover hidden truths. Telestreet was not about discovering technical innovations or new media languages.

Above all, Telestreet was a political campaign against the power that has been illegally concentrated in the hands of a media-financial company. It was also a practical critique of the communicative system that is condensed within television. The important result that Telestreet achieved was the activation of a large number of people who organized themselves into media activist groups, mobilized with their agitating recording tools and experimented with whatever was at hand in order to acquire technical and political skills in microbroadcasting, thus setting in motion processes of social self-organization of one sector of cognitive work.

We cannot say if, in the body of the experiments performed by the various street

TVs, there were new stylistic inventions, that new forms or new languages were created. It is possible, but until this moment we have not focused on this. Is this a limit to the experiment? Perhaps, but the point is this: since the beginning of this experiment, the intent of Bolognese media activists has been focused entirely on how the technocommunicative system and the politics of its operation could represent the social imaginary of contemporary Italy. The question was how to capture and share the spirit behind the street-TV network, which was the spirit of an epoch that no longer had any faith in power or in politics, and perhaps no hope for the future. This was (and still is) an epoch characterized by people who realize that they are alone, yet who are unable to square themselves with the irreparable catastrophe carving out a ground zero in their lives, and above all in the collective life of global humanity. The media activists behind the OrfeoTV experiment realized how worthwhile it was to collect the tools available to them, to connect friends who came out of corners, to go on the attack barehanded, without the hope of winning, but with the certainty of doing the only thing that one can do. Resist the homogenized horror, avoid the imaginary of submission, refuse the glossy hypocrisy and put into motion bizarre systems and unpredictable connections. This was what OrfeoTV was meant to be: a non-homogenized imaginative machine. Then the wars started.

The Vision of the Horror

The beginning of this century was marked by the explosion of a mad aggression. Since September 11, 2001, war has become routine; indeed it has become the horizon beyond which no one is able to see. A war that has been presented by both sides as interminable, preventative and merciless—two sides, by the way, which closely resemble one another. The war has naturally become the focus of street-TV stations because media activist groups have participated in the mobilization of the peace movement: they went to interview schoolchildren and the elderly in retirement homes about the war on terrorism, and they filmed the candle-lit vigils at nighttime and the daytime marches with multicolored banners.

At a certain point, many street-TV stations decided to form, if only temporarily, a satellite television channel against the war. It was not an easy decision or one taken lightly. In fact, the implicit model of the Telestreet experiment was not easily reducible to the model of satellite television. Telestreet meant the proliferation of micro-TV stations through the transformation of regular receiving antennas into transmitters, and sought to reticulate the diffusion of electronic video images. Satellite broadcasting, on the other hand, required the creation of a central production agency able to select, edit and screen the available material; its goal was to reach a large and geographically diffuse audience.

The creation of a satellite television channel dedicated to protesting the politics of war necessarily implied the belief that there was a lack of information or a truth deficit that the regime's television was responsible for creating and maintaining. It implied the intention to fill this void, to respond to the demand for truth that the regime's television, by its nature, could not and would not respond to. The Telestreet model did not at all conform with this "counterinformation" idea. Telestreet was not counterinformation, but a way out of the world of referential meaning. This problem was examined and discussed many times in the meetings that preceded the linking of the Telestreet network to the No War satellite channel. In the end, not everyone agreed with the decision to join that initiative.

On December 10, 2002, Emergency, an Italian NGO founded by Italian physicians working in war zones, organized a No War Day, with the mobilization of protests in all cities, candlelight vigils, and sit-ins. For the day, it rented eight hours of time on a satellite television channel. This made it possible to broadcast the day's events (interviews, meetings, marches) all over the country. Global TV was born out of this experience, and began to broadcast on a satellite channel shortly thereafter.

In the first months of 2003, when the drums of war were rumbling and the heroic Western military divisions were preparing the slaughter, Italian media activism thought it necessary to prepare informational tools in order to shed light on a war that they feared would be carried out in the dark, without witnesses, without images. They believed the war televisions would hide the reality of the massacre. That assumption turned out to be mistaken.

From the moment the bombardments of Iraqi territory began, the entire world was drowned in horrifying images. Decapitated bodies, houses with their windows blown out and all the things inside blackened by smoke, wretched people who screamed with terror in their eyes, blood and dust—everything was documented. In 1991, the images of the first American war against the Iraqi regime had been shot from the point of view of smart bombs in search of their targets, and had all the cool cleanness of an electronic interface and the dissociated passion of the video game. This time, the horror was shown in all its terrifying truth, clashing with the words of the Western warriors who in Doha, Washington or London spoke in euphoric tones of the advance of the liberators.

However strong the political-military control of information, the effect was very different from what we had expected. Journalists, for the most part, behaved as workers who want to do their work decently, and they narrated the horror they encountered day by day, hour by hour. But these journalists wound up victims of the strong polarization between those who were following the occupation forces and the rest of the press.

The American government had in fact given a considerable number of trusted American journalists access to the battlefield, and this was unprecedented in the recent history of war journalism. These embedded journalists, in exchange for being allowed to follow the combatants up close, voluntarily submitted to a series of restrictions on their reporting freedoms. The U.S. Defense Department (Rumsfeld and his men) had thought up this particular solution to prevent accusations of a media blackout similar to the one during the first Gulf War, and at the same time to be able to maintain tight control over information. With the embedded journalists (for the most part shortened to "embeds," which sounds curiously similar to "in bed") the Pentagon compelled American journalists to submit to a strict self-censorship, to limit themselves to describing situations in a very generic manner, to refrain from mentioning the weapons used by their own troops, and to obey the orders of the commanding officer of the unit to which they were assigned. This officer could declare at any moment a media freeze or confiscate their cell phone (with the excuse that a transmission could reveal the unit's position to the enemy). With the embeds, American reporters were for the first time intimate participants in the military's actions and encounters. This generated excited and propagandist information, with journalists clothed in protective vests and night-vision goggles ecstatically admiring the power, speed and precision of the American deployments. A clear linguistic symptom of this embrace on the nuptial bed of war was the substitution of the third-person pronoun "they" with the more inclusive "we," thus seriously compromising the self-image of the reporter as someone able to express critical-analytic judgments on the situation.

This situation had two principal effects: the construction of particularly factious information by the embeds; and a structural (and dangerous) division between embeds (essentially American journalists) and all the others (Reporters sans Frontières estimated that of the 2,000–2,500 journalists present in and around Iraq, only 600 were embedded).

On the one hand, this divide reduced the danger that all the information provided would be reduced to propaganda; more diverse and global news was possible (primarily due to the presence of Arab journalists). On the other hand, it left this second group of journalists less protected, and thus more vulnerable to attacks from both sides.

The American military distinguished itself in a series of attacks on nonembedded journalists, for example, the attack on the Palestine Hotel in Baghdad (official headquarters of the nonaligned press) that caused the death of Taras Protsyuk, a Ukrainian cameraman who worked for Reuters, and of José Couso, a Spanish cameraman. American troops also bombed the offices of Al Jazeera and Abu Dhabi Television, killing Tareq Ayyoub, a Jordanian-Palestinian journalist who worked for Al Jazeera (let us not forget that the offices of Al Jazeera were already bombed by American planes during the war on Afghanistan in 2001).

Both the American military and the Iraqi regime tried to marginalize and repress the independence of journalists, but the principle of competition between the various new agencies made it impossible to cancel out diverging voices, and at least outside of the United States, this facilitated the dissemination of information broad enough to permit a clear understanding of what was really happening: a succession of heinous crimes and the beginning of a long-term war.

This did not mean that the information system told "the truth," it meant only that the sanitization of information about the war in many countries (above all in Arab countries and in Europe) did not succeed, thanks to a sort of spontaneous revolt by news agents who had the courage to report what they saw. Even information channels subject to the control of the information regime, such as RAI, ended up providing contradictory and clashing views of the situation. The packaging of the programs was sugar-coated, falsified, triumphalist and sanitized, but every once in a while the correspondents (above all the female correspondents) would speak in their own voice, with their own gestures and their own words, and the horrors they witnessed came through. The ridiculous talking heads of the national news programs (both on RAI and Berlusconi's networks) chirped reassuring words about the advance of the troops who brought liberation to a people oppressed by supreme evil, but when the faces of Giovanna Botteri in Baghdad and other female journalists in other war zones appeared, we were able to understand what was really going on, and the crust of hypocrisy was repeatedly broken.

The information blackout forecasted by Italian media activists did not happen, why? Why had the powers that be allowed the European television-viewing public to bear witness to the intolerable? We could propose various hypotheses, such as an error in the American estimation of the Iraqi resistance, or the willingness and desire of the majority of journalists to generate independent information. One might even suppose that the feeling of repugnance the broadcasted violence prompted in the majority of viewers was no longer very important to the powers that be. Indeed, these powers were no longer preoccupied with obtaining the consensus of the Western populace: instead they were intent on provoking terror, which generated a supine acceptance of any violence: "Let them do anything, commit any violence as long as it is not directed against me, as long as I can be spared."

In the end, what lesson did we learn from months and months of viewing the horror on a daily basis? Perhaps it is too soon to say, because the systematic power displayed in those months may still be working deeply on the global unconscious, carving a trench of hatred in the heart of an entire generation and pushing millions of youth, and not just Arabs, to plot revenge with merciless methods. There was one thing that appeared fairly clear early on: the vision of the horror, the exhibition of illegitimate force that can destroy everything and (apparently) obtain everything, paralyzed the will and oppressed the soul with such a load of disgust that the desire to protest, to demonstrate peacefully, to declare in the light of day the rights of civil and political life, seemed to be exhausted.

More than once the White House declared all that which did not follow its will to power to be irrelevant. They threatened the United Nations and the European Union, declaring those institutions that did not follow their will to war to be irrelevant. "He who does not accept the dictate of force no longer counts," proclaimed the lords of war. The spectacle produced by the mastiffs in London and Washington (and their puppies in Rome and Warsaw) was one of absolute arrogance. Military brutality was shown to be the only source of right, of law and even of reality. The vision of horror, the systematic exhibition of the suffering of the weak, the humiliation of those who did not possess hypertechnological weapons: this spectacle of power that knew no reason functioned as a very powerful dissuader. Negotiations were good for nothing, reason was good for nothing, culture was good for nothing, beauty was good for nothing, so too with love, prayer and the word. The only thing that was good for something was power.

This message flowed from the uninterrupted viewing of horror. This was the dissuasive and paralyzing message that could result in a prolonged depression of civil society and the underground formation of an army of hate and revenge.

Media activists should reflect on this experience. It was no longer the job of media activism to inform, to unmask and to show. Everything there was to see, we saw. Everything there was to know, we knew. The result was that we were no longer able to imagine, nor to desire, nor to hope for anything.

We must recognize that one of the premises on which Italian media activism based the satellite television initiative of No War/Global TV was belied: the idea that there would only be very restricted information on the war provided to the global public proved untrue. Did we think that more images, more blood, more dust, more terror than what we were able to view would have been useful?

Conclusion

As Deleuze and Guattari said, and is true more than ever today: "We do not lack communication. On the contrary, we have too much of it. We lack creation. We lack resistance to the present" (1994: 108). What is missing is political, linguistic and communicative creation. The ability to respond to horror with an efficient mobilization is missing. Tens of millions of people protested all over the world, but it was not enough. Street-TV stations followed the protests with their cameras, filmed the marches, interviewed thousands of people, got people to talk and broadcast the faces and voices of pacifists. But it did not serve any purpose, or at least it was not enough.

The acceleration, the overload and the angst of the conflict come to nothing, though they were probably inevitable. Perhaps, one thinks, in such situations it would be better pull the plug and not participate in the flow, to take a step away from the surrounding media frenzy.

We must reflect on this: what innovation can we make on the narrative level? How can we create zones of social existence that do not suffer the essential impoverishment and the psychological and physical violence of war? Only if we are able to produce something political on this level (that of content, style and narrative invention) will we have produced something complete and useful.

We are midway though our work. Street TVs are not interested in competing at the crammed level of information, in taking up space in the already super-saturated ether. Rather, these stations should work toward the creation of a recognizable sign that does not preach peace, but constructs friendship, because peace is not the effective opposite of war. Peace dissolves as soon as a bully fires his cannon. Friendship endures, underground and invincible, and does not collapse under the blackmail of war. Telestreet must become communication for friendship.

conclusion

The Emergence of a Post-Media Sensibility

In the preface to his book on the Italian radio movement published in 1977, Felix Guattari writes: "The police destroyed Radio Alice; its producers have been either forced into exile or arrested, found guilty, and imprisoned; the radio station's materials have been sacked and impounded. However, Radio Alice's revolutionary work with its bent on deterritorialization continues throughout the nervous system of its executioners" (Guattari 1977: iii).

In an essay aptly entitled "*Des Millions d'Alice en Puissance*" [Millions and Millions of Potential Alices], Guattari describes Radio Alice as being much more than a tool for information: it was a mechanism that contributed to the dismantling of the monolithic Italian mass media system. Such a dismantling was the logical consequence of the reclamation of the communicative public sphere by social movements in the 1960s and 1970s. The struggles of those years started the systematic restructuring of the center nodes of the establishment's nervous system, and this process continued over the next decades with some important victories, but too many catastrophic defeats.

What sparked Guattari's interest in the alternative radio movement was not simply its practice of counterinformation, but especially its ability to develop and broadcast a prodigious array of voices and perspectives. Guattari believed that this proliferation of communicative agents would eventually lead to the explosion of the mass media system. Well before the World Wide Web became a concrete reality, he foresaw a post-mass-media civilization just beyond the horizon: a civilization where communicative flows were no longer directed from above toward a passive audience, but traveled within the thick, horizontal web of rhizomatic exchanges set up by equally empowered agents. The 'web' had always been Guattari's favorite model of reference, even before this word acquired the meaning it has today. With his concept of the rhizome, he anticipated the technonomadic reality of the Web. When Guattari died in 1992, the Internet was just in its infancy. He never witnessed how in the following years it would transform the global communicative system by introducing rhizomatic paths of communication, thus weakening the mass media's centric model.

Mass media can be used as tools for amplifying human abilities and function as extensions of the body. Too often, modern mass media have been used to disempower human agency, stripping people of their ability to imagine a different world and subjugating human creativity to the interests of powerful elites. For instance, radio allows for a boundless extension of the human voice, yet in the political conditions of the twentieth century, radio became the amplification of the master's voice while simultaneously annihilating and minimizing the voice of civic society. "Hate radios" proliferated throughout the world—from Nazi Germany, which provided all households with radio receivers so that Hitler's voice would fill all ears, to the Rwandan genocide in 1994, where Radio Télévision Libre des Milles Collines disseminated hate propaganda inciting the murder of Tutsis and opponents to the Hutu regime, greatly contributing to the slaughter of hundreds of thousands of people.

From the start, media activists have posed the question of how to disentangle the mass media from the oppressive power strategies that have historically possessed it and determined its modalities. A potential answer to this question comes from looking at mass media as manifestations of the Foucauldian concept of *dispositif*. For Foucault, dispositifs are "thoroughly heterogeneous ensembles" of discursive and material elements, "multilinear ensembles composed of heterogeneous lines," with power, knowledge and subjectivity comprising the major variables. It is the complex set of relations of these dispositifs which allows us to see and speak, establishing grids of intelligibility and, in the process, producing their own truths. Dispositifs constitute the horizon of the world (the limits of our thought and action), expressing the weight, corporeality and power of being. Yet all dispositifs reject unbreakable and definitive contours. They always leak. Processes of subjectification can easily become lines of flight.

McLuhan's analysis of the media (in particular his privileging of medium over content) suggests an understanding of the mass media as *unbreakable dispositifs*, which in turn could lead to a paralyzing technological determinism. If we view the mass media as *leaking dispositifs*, we can still imagine that the media shape the social, imaginary and cultural domains—but this happens through a multiplicity of social and cultural semiotic lines, not all of them drawn by the dominant hegemony.

While we acknowledge that the use and function of the media is necessarily linked to its structure, we want to point out that this structural relation cannot be traced back to a single design. We can imagine media practices that are autonomous from would-be inescapable dispositifs in the techno-media production: "There is nothing that is major or revolutionary except the minor," wrote Deleuze and Guattari in *Kafka: Toward a Minor Literature* (1986: 26). The minor is not the minority, for the simple fact that it encompasses a potential multitude. At any given time, it could start multiplying itself, take flight along unexpected lines of escape or develop a recombinant principle able to shift an entire paradigm.

Independent media proposes to damage the media dispositifs themselves and develop lines of escape away from the practices of media regimes—above all, away from the political imperatives that manufacture consent in the user. Let's take for example the television: it is used to shape people into spectators; into passive receivers of a hypnotic and oneiric flow. The technical-structural linkage between broadcast station and home reception, cathode tube and TV room, is part of a power technology producing a dispositif that does not only serve ideological, discursive or commodified content but also shapes social relations, communicative behavior and linguistic choices. As the Telestreet experience shows, even the television dispositif can be traversed by lines of independent communication and can function as a recombinant agent. Through these low-power broadcast stations and their networks, television became a medium for the construction of a web of near-vision dissent, based on local production, interactivity and real-time feedback loops.

The phenomena described in this book as "media activism" intend to produce lines of flight out of media dispositifs that have been structured to encourage political apathy. Italian media activism did not want to use mass media to provide "better information" or "better content": it wanted to fake the media at its structural level; it wanted to sabotage the linkages and the interfaces that gave rise to unbreakable, monolithic dispositifs.

The media experiences explored in this book (Radio Alice, Rekombinant.org, Telestreet) owe their successes to their ability to transform the taken-for-granted functioning of the media into alternative practices, and in finding social uses for them. Italian media activists understood that in order to succeed they could not simply exist as alternatives to the dominant media outlets (which in the last twenty years meant Berlusconi's networks). If they tried to simply resist the dominant media by force, or by oppositional content, they would have failed. These groups understood that they needed to invent a social communication based on irony, deviance, disorder and otherness. They sought to let the obscene emerge ("that which cannot be seen") and act as proliferating agents for lines of flight from the media dispositifs—ones that could potentially lead to social change.

This is our wish for the future of media activism: that it be more than simple resistance in a struggle to "speak truth to power," but rather that it develop into a minor able to produce millions of molecular social agents ('*des millions d'Alice en puissance*') and put forward a communicative logic based on an alterity that is incompatible with the power and practices of media regimes.

conclusion

Postface to the English Edition

What has changed in Italy in the last few years? This book was written between 2001 and 2006, when Italy was ruled by Berlusconi. It contains an analysis of the political and media activism of that period, and reconstructs the cultural and mediatic scenarios in which the *Berlusconismo* prospered. In the meantime, Italy kept developing surreal scenarios, such as the 2006 national elections, where a center-left coalition guided by Romano Prodi defeated the center-right block led by Berlusconi by an extremely small margin (less than 24,000 ballots).

By the end of 2007 things were still evolving, and it is indeed quite probable that the Italian situation will mutate again before this book is in the bookstores. To document the Italian political twists and turns is always a difficult enterprise, because the political scenarios keep changing: new parties are born; governments fall before their term expires; corruption spreads in spite of the judiciary efforts in the last decade; and every day, new catastrophes are announced only to be dismissed the day after.

At the same time, we could say that the situation has not changed at all. What changed in the last power transfer from the government guided by Silvio Berlusconi to the one guided by Romano Prodi? Very little.

When the center-left finally won the elections in 2006 we expected some change: laws to regulate the conflict of interest between media conglomerates and political parties; reforms of the television system; reforms of revenue transfers to help the working class; a revamping of the public school system, seriously wounded by cuts inflicted by the center-right agenda with its favoring of private schools.

But in the first two years of the new government, those expectations have been completely disattended. At the very least, did the social agenda change? It did not. Even in this government, with its forces that call themselves "reformist" and others that claim continuity with the old communist tradition, the political decisions starkly resemble the ones made by the Berlusconi regime; they share the same agenda to produce a neoliberal, securitarian state. After all the electoral chatter cleared, we found out that the polar star of Prodi's government is the same one that guided Berlusconi: reduction of labor costs, revenue transfers from labor to profit, tax rebates for the enterprises and reduction of social expenditures.

If nothing changed on the social agenda, even less changed in media politics, the main battlefield of conflict and protest when Berlusconi was prime minister. Because of the weakness of the Prodi coalition (it does not have a solid majority and must continuously deal with the danger of defections from members of his coalition), in the past two years, the government has not been able to introduce a legislative plan on the conflict of interest, and it has not been able to propose a reform of the media system. Consequently, Berlusconi's media power, which had been strengthened by the legislative activity of his past governments, has not been touched by the new government. It has been cowed into delaying any debate on the topic.

What's more, during the spring of 2007, Silvio Berlusconi, the owner of Mediaset, Forza Italia president, and temporarily dethroned monarch, has been able to widen his already omnipotent media power by coming up with a scheme that he would have never dared to concoct while prime minister.

Mediaset, the media conglomerate owned by Berlusconi, acquired Endimol, a company that produces television formats of different kinds (above all reality shows) and sells them to RAI, the public company that manages the three television channels which should theoretically compete with Mediaset.

What does this mean? It means that Mediaset, already the dominant player in the Italian mediascape, has become even more powerful, up to the point of gaining access to, and determining the production of its main competitor. In absence of a law that regulates these kinds of conflicts of interest and curbs any monopolistic attempts in the media field, the person who has the de facto control of the media—that is, Berlusconi—can do whatever he wants.

Video-Blogging and the End of Telestreet

When Berlusconi was in power, media-activists created novel ways to counteract his monopoly and shape new forms of resistance. In this book we explored the experience of Telestreet as it unfolded between 2002 and 2004. By 2006, that experience was exhausted. The reasons for the demise of the Telestreet experiment are multiple.

The media activists who gave life to that movement did not have financial backing, and the experience of production and transmission was sustained entirely by their volunteered efforts. After a few years, fatigue took hold and many Telestreet outlets closed down. Another, perhaps more important, reason for the changes in the Italian activist mediascape and the decline of Telestreet: the emergence of Web 2.0, and above all, the emergence of video-blogging.

Seven years ago, a video activist who wanted to broadcast her products had to invest her energies in the creation and management of a micro-TV station. This allowed her to reach a little more than a few hundred people who lived in close proximity to the station. Thanks to broadband Internet and video-blogging websites, youtube.com among them, today a young video activist can address a far less homogenous (at least from a territorial point of view) and infinitely wider audience.

The development of the convergence process—that is, the progressive transfer of all media production into online environments—is producing a deep mutation in contemporary mediascapes; one that will revolutionize the way the next generation of media activists will operate. This change is affecting all media production, from radio to video.

The first Italian pirate radio stations were an expression of the need to communicate content that wasn't covered by the monopolistic broadcasts of the Italian state. The experience of Telestreet was still tied to this same imperative: since the teledictatorship occupied all available spaces, it was necessary to open new areas of expression, and broadcasting over the shadow cones appeared as one possibility to increase the sphere of independent production. Thus, prior to video-blogs, the history of independent communication and media activism has been shaped by the struggle to gain a space from which to speak.

The Problem for the Next Wave of Independent Media

In the present scenario, where anyone has access to media production and distribution via online services, the main concern is no longer one of open access.

The free radio movement emerged out of the communicative desert of the 1970s, whereas Web radios are borne from an extremely dense panorama of cacophonic voices. In the same way, video activists today have expressive channels like youtube or thousand of other video-blogs that render the mediascape an immensely crowded space. The problem today is no longer one of freedom of expression, but perhaps its exact opposite: the right to silence. We no longer suffer from what was once upon a time called censorship; to the contrary, we suffer from the uninterrupted flow of stimuli that we are less and less able to decipher critically. Modern dictatorships were generally based on censorship: their aim was to silence alternative voices in order to impose only one voice, and to create an atmosphere of consent around that voice. Late-modern totalitarian systems are no longer based on censorship, but on white noise.

The passage from an authoritarian system based on persuasive messages (as were the totalitarian regimes of the twentieth century) to a system based on pervasive messages (like the contemporary info-dictatorship) has been characterized by the acceleration and multiplication of broadcasted messages.

The former systems were founded on consent: citizens had to understand the reasons of their leader; a single source of information was authorized; dissenting voices were censored. The contemporary info-dictatorship owes its power to sensory overload: the acceleration and proliferation of the semiotic flows reach a terminal velocity where only white noise is left; all content is lost in myriad indistinguishable, indecipherable or irrelevant messages.

The Internet not only produces technical innovations, but also transforms the relationship between sender and listener, and weakens the communicative power of both radio and television media. This is the new scenario facing contemporary media activism: how to remain significant in a world drowning in signs, data trash and media pollution.

Is there any hope for a positive mutation? When we started this book, and up until three or four years ago, we would have answered that hope lies in the autonomy of social movements, in the autonomous organization of social processes, and in particular, in the autonomous organization of media production. Is this still true?

Bibliography

Albert, M. 1993. *Capitalism vs. Capitalism*. London: Four Walls Eight Windows. [1991. *Capitalisme Contre Capitalisme*. Paris: Editions du Seuil.]

Banfield, E. 1958. *The Moral Basis of a Backward Society*. New York: Free Press.

Baranski, Z. and West, R. (eds.) 2001. *The Cambridge Companion to Modern Italian Culture*. Cambridge, UK: Cambridge University Press.

Barthes, R. 1978 [1977]. *A Lover's Discourse*. New York: Farrar, Strauss and Giroux.

Baudrillard, J. 1981 [1972]. *Toward a Critique of the Political Economy of the Sign*. St. Louis, MO: Telos.

Baudrillard, J. 1993 [1976]. *Symbolic Exchange and Death*. London: Sage Publications.

Blondet, Maurizio. 1995. *Elogio di Catilina e Berlusconi*. Milan: Il Cerchio.

Bocca, Giorgio. 2003. *Piccolo Cesare*. Milan: Feltrinelli.

Bourdieu, P. 1979. *Algeria 1960*. Cambridge, UK: Cambridge University Press.

Calabrese, 0. 1975. *Carosello o dell'educazione serale*. Florence: Cooperativa Libraria Universitaria.

Calabrese, O. 1991. *L'età neobarocca*. Bari: Laterza.

Cavalli, A. 2001. "Reflections on Political Culture and the 'Italian National Character.'" *Daedalus*, Vol. 130.

Colombo, F. and Padellaro, A. 2002. *Il libro nero della democrazia. Vivere sotto il governo Berlusconi*. Milan: Baldini Castoldi Dalai.

Cordero, F. 2003. *Le strane regole del signor B*. Milan: Garzanti.

Debord, G. 1994 [1967]. *The Society of the Spectacle*. New York: Zone Books.

Deleuze, G. 1990 [1969]. *The Logic of Sense*. New York: Columbia University Press.

Bibliography

Deleuze, G. and Guattari, F. 1977 [1972]. *Anti-Oedipus: Capitalism and Schizophrenia*. London: Penguin.

Deleuze, G. and Guattari, F. 1986 [1975]. *Kafka: Toward a Minor Literature*. Minneapolis: University of Minnesota Press.

Deleuze, G. and Guattari, F. 1986 [1980]. *Nomadology: The War Machine*. New York: Semiotext(e).

Deleuze, G. and Guattari, F. 1994 [1991]. *What is Philosophy?* New York: Columbia University Press.

Foucault, M. 1965 [1961]. *Madness and Civilization*. London: Penguin.

Foucault, M. 1972 [1969]. *The Archaeology of Knowledge*. London: Penguin.

Foucault, M. 1977 [1975]. *Discipline and Punish*. London: Penguin.

Gilder, G. 1990. *Life After Television: The Coming Transformation of Media and American Life*. New York: Norton.

Ginsborg, P. 1990. *A History of Contemporary Italy: Society and Politics, 1943–88*. London: Penguin.

Ginsborg, P. 2003. *Italy and Its Discontents: Family, Civil Society, State*. London: Palgrave Macmillan.

Ginsborg, P. 2004. *Berlusconi: Television, Power, and Patronimy*. London: Verso.

Goldsen, R. 1977. *The Show and Tell Machine*. New York: Doubleday.

Guattari, F. 1977. In Collectif A/Traverso (ed.). *Radio Alice, Radio Libre*. Paris: De Large.

Greenfield, P. M. 1984. *Mind and Media: The Effects of Television, Video Games, and Computers*. Cambridge, MA: Harvard University Press.

Iyer, P. 1989. *Video Night in Katmandu*. London: Black Swan.

Bibliography

Jones, T. 2003. *The Dark Heart of Italy*. New York: North Point Press.

Levinson, P. 1997. *The Soft Edge: A Natural History and Future of the Information Revolution*. London, New York: Routledge.

Lucidi, M. 2002. *Le mani sulla cultura*. Rome: Malatempora.

Marazzi, C. 2002. *Capitale e linguaggio*. Rome: Derive Approdi.

Mirzoeff, N. 1999. *An Introduction to Visual Culture*. London, New York: Routledge.

Negus, G. 2002. *The World from Italy: Football, Food and Politics*. Melbourne: HarperCollins Australia.

Schneider, J. and Schneider, P. 1976. *Culture and Political Economy in Western Sicily*. New York: Academic Press.

Stille, A. 2007. *The Sack of Rome, How Silvio Berlusconi Took Over Italy*. London: Penguin.

Torrealta, M. 2002. *La trattativa*. Rome: Editori Riuniti.

Travaglio, M. 2001. *L'odore dei soldi*. Rome: Editori Riuniti.

Tuccari, F. (ed.) 2002. *Il Governo Berlusconi tra promesse e realtà*. Rome: Laterza.

Weber, M. 2002 [1930]. *The Protestant Ethic and the Spirit of Capitalism*. London: Routledge.